Insights For The Senior's Ministry

Understanding The Myths & Truths Of The Aging Process

Dr. Joseph R. Rogers, Sr.

Dedication

Dedicated to my dear Mother, **Pearlie Graham Rogers**, who birthed, reared and nourished me into what I am today. A dear, sweet, Godly lady who speaks loud with closed lips and who teaches without any formal education.

Dedicated to my darling wife, **Lola Mae (Vick) Rogers (2008)**, who has given me the joy of living in a relationship that words them-selves cannot justify. For her caring and support, I am most grateful.

Joseph R. Rogers, Sr., D. Min.

Table Of Contents

	Page No.
1. Introduction	6
2. The Views On Aging	12
Historically	12
Theologically	15
Sociologically	22
Educationally	25
3. Aging	35
Demographics	35
Understanding Special Terms In Aging	37
Stereotypes, Myths, Ageism	38
4. Elderly Concerns	49
Economics of Aging	49
Living Arrangements For The Elderly	53
Legal Aspects	58
5. Psychological Aspects of Aging	62
Mental Disorders	62
Functional Disorders	63
Organic Brain Disorders	65

   Alzheimer's Disease------------------------------ 69
   Depression--- 70

6. Biological Aging--- 75
   Biological Aging Of The Body Systems---------- 76
   Dermal System------------------------------------ 76
   Musculoskeletal System-------------------------- 78
   Cardiovascular System--------------------------- 79
   Respiratory System------------------------------- 80
   Gastrointestinal System-------------------------- 81
   Renal System-------------------------------------- 81
   Reproductive System----------------------------- 81
   Immune System----------------------------------- 82
   Nervous System----------------------------------- 83
   Impotence--- 86

7. Coming of Age-- 88
   Aging Has Come of Age------------------------- 88
   Reactions To Coming Of Age-------------------- 90

8. Biblical Perspectives On Aging--------------------------- 92
   Biblical Perspectives For Understanding Aging-- 92
   Personal Bible Perspectives----------------------- 95

9. Death And Dying --- 100
      Death In Greek And Old Testament Thought ------ 101
      Death In The New Testament ----------------------- 103
      Acceptance Of Death ----------------------------------- 104
      Causes Of Death --------------------------------------- 106
      Grief And Its Stages ---------------------------------- 111
      Fear Of Death -- 112
      Activities Concerning Death Of The Aging ----------- 116
      Effective Caring Attitudes ----------------------------- 117

10. Conclusions --- 121
      Selected Bibliography --------------------------------- 122
      Update --- 125
      Author's Contracts And Other Works --------------- 128
      Notes -- 129

Chapter 1

Introduction

During August 1984, The United States Department of Commerce Revealed there are 27.4 million people aged sixty-five and over living in the United States.[1] Two-thirds of this number live in families of some type and one-third, mainly widowed females, live entirely alone. Statistics reflect that we are becoming a country of aged people and the life expectancy of women is longer than men's.

This is not an entirely new situation because the average age of our population has been increasing since 1900. If the trend continues, by the year two thousand there will be 34 to 35 million people who are over sixty-five years of age in America. Consequently, with these chronological facts in front of us, we as a nation are going to have to examine our priorities in dealing with aged people. These people will be you and I.

It is projected if we continue on the same collision course with our Social Security system, during the 1990s there will be two individuals paying Social Security taxes to take care of one retired person. Many concerns are being examined by our so-called experts in the field of gerontology.

More aged persons not only have a sociological impact on the country as a whole, but on the church as well. Church leadership in its ministry to and with this group of persons needs to understand the implications brought about by their increasing number. In the past we have thought of the middle aged people doing ministry with the children, youth, and those who have reached the age of sixty –five or over.

However, since persons sixty-five or over, coupled with those over fifty-five, are becoming the more dominant group within the church, we're going to have to rethink our priorities in ministry. We must realize that the is no retirement in God's economy until we reach the time when we are called to our eternal residence or are prevented from doing ministry because of physiological and psychological reasons. We must as a church recycle our thinking and begin to understand that when people reach a certain age, be it sixty-five or older, this doesn't mean they should be placed on a shelf and thought of as helpless or non-contributing members.

Every person, if physically possible, needs to be incorporated into the ministry arm of the church. We must begin a program of psychologically preparing and training persons for ministry during their senior years. If not, we are going to have a group of people sixty-five or over, the majority in many church bodies, not doing what they should be equipped to do. The overall result would be that many churches would perform little effective ministry.

In many, if not most, of our churches, the members of the fifty-five to sixty-five and up category probably represent about twenty-five percent of those enrolled within the church, and more than likely those numbers are equally divided between the fifty-five to sixty-five and the sixty-five age group rightly expect to live well beyond sixty-five. This fact, coupled with our slower birth rate, will cause the church to have a higher percentage of those over sixty-five in the future.

The church which I presently pastor has a church school enrollment of 300. Approximately eighty of this number are senior adults, with ages roughly equally divided between the fifty-five to sixty-five and the over sixty-five groups. They represent the largest amount of giving within the church and the greatest percentage in attendance on any given Sunday. They really are the power group within the church. If they took it upon themselves to exercise their potential ministry, our church would have a much greater influence on the community.

In other words, they had no desire to be shelved or placed aside and just be ministered to. They wanted to be actively involved in the ministry. Consequently, even though our church should provide the physical means of transportation and visitation and fellowship, I felt an additional need to equip this great source of "people power" for ministry.

I felt a need to design and implement a project which would prepare our senior adults for ministry. What does this problem have to do with my ministry during this time and in this space? For me to be caring is one thing, but to be caring and effectively helpful is another. I can reach out and touch someone in need; this reveals a caring attitude, and the person I touch may feel my empathy and support.

However, that person receives little help in the practical area. For instance, if a lonely widow needs a hot lunch, she requires more than an "I understand" and a short prayer. I need to be informed so I can share how the local Meals on Wheels operates or where she can drive t get a subsidized nutritious meal. In order to answer questions from senior adults, I need to be informed about these services and other helping agencies within our community.

In addition, the individual aging person sometimes falls prey to the myths and stereotypes of our uninformed culture and assumes the expected role or roles. A minister should be prepared to inform this needful person that the so-called "truths" about the aging process are in reality unfounded. Through acquired knowledge, the minister should be able to explode these myths with factual information.

Many of our senior adults are not aware of all the governmental social programs which can offer assistance to them. A very small percentage of senior adults take advantage of many programs designed to meet their basic needs. These programs go beyond the Social Security, Medicare and Medicaid. Many programs are not on a "justified need" basis; they're available to all over sixty-five. A minister needs to be aware of these agencies so he can share information about them with needful senior adults.

Therefore, to minister effectively in today's world, the local pastor needs some understanding of the physiological, sociological, economical and theological needs of the senior adult within the church. He should also be aware of the helps available within the individual agencies.

There is no way in the local church that I can on a one-to-one basis share the information with each needful senior adult. However, I believe this problem can be solved. If I as pastor/teacher prepare the senior saints by sharing the information in a group process I have gleaned from different resources, not only will they be informed, but they can also become helpers. By having some understanding of the aging process, these seniors will have their needs met, and in turn, they can possibly help others' needs by sharing.

If just the myths and stereotypes about ageism that have been internalized over the years can be eliminated, they will have a better understanding of their aging process.

Having known some of the participants for a period of time, I feel that when the seniors converse with their peers, they will share in an informal manner their new insights about aging. This is one of the ways that the Christian witness is taken into the market place. Enlightened senior adults n these one-on-one encounters will be sharing will be sharing with persons who would never agree to a classroom experience. In this manner some understanding of the aging process will reach other senior adults in our church and in the community.

By participating in this learning experience, the senior adults' self-esteem will be buttressed. Also, they will have that unexplainable feeling of Christian joy as they perform ministry to a fellow believer or to a potential believer. My ministry will be enhanced by understanding some of the needs of senior adults and by equipping some of these senior adults to help me in doing ministry in the local church. The Bible clearly teaches that we are all ministers. We all have gifts, even the gift of service. The overall purpose of this book will be to prepare senior adults for stewardship through an understanding of the aging process.

At the conclusion of the book, hopefully, you will understand the aging process; affirm worth as individuals; realize their potential for intellectual growth and personal development; identify programs and agencies established as service agencies for senior adults; share gained information with other senior adults; and deal responsibly with numerous opportunities, experiences, and needs; i.e. death and dying, grief, sexuality, nutrition, mental health, Social Security, Medicare, Medicaid, finances, physical security, primary relationships, and volunteerism. If the objectives are accomplished, senior adults should have a basic understanding of the aging process.

The information shared will be for the most part general, sometimes specific, but at no time more technical more technical than necessary. Gerontology is a relatively new field of intense study; consequently, even the information available has not been tested by longitudinal studies.

Chapter 1
Endnotes

1. Pictogram, "Spotlight On Older Americans," *U.S. News & World Report*, 2 July 1984, p. 53.

Chapter 2
Views On Aging

Historically

The aging process or being aged has been viewed from different perspectives in recorded history. In Old Testament writings the aged person was treated with respect and honor. The aged male was the head of his family or clan until he relinquished leadership because of incapacitation or death. In all matters of importance, elders were consulted. The life span began to level off at about 120 years toward the end of Genesis.

Life span is the maximum years of the human life. The life span generally accepted by today's gerontologist is 110 to 120 years. The oldest documented human life span in the United States is 114 years. In Japan it is documented that a man lived to the age of 118.

Aged persons had an important role in the Old Testament history. Because of their attitudes toward aging, we should learn some lessons for our contemporary society:

> "If there is truth in what some of us believe, mainly that the biblical literature as a whole breathes the breath of the Almighty, then it is also true that a large portion of this breath breathes in and through the mind of its old people. And as the breath of the Almighty touches us through their minds, they are ours, and we are theirs."[1]

The early church (first five hundred years) looked after the material necessities for the elderly; they also gave them important roles in the community; consequently, they had venerated status. The early Greek and Roman cultures also venerated their elders. The father had complete control over his family until his death, regardless of the family members' ages. The older men were the leaders and the wise men of their culture. Early America seems to have held the aged person in high regard also. Martin Marty examines early society's feeling toward older people:

"Those who have any familiarity with historical records about the aged in early America – say, from 1492 until almost 1892 – almost never see age – specific references about old people being a problem. How the problem came to be discerned or invented, whether the process was gradual or sudden, or whether certain events or persons produced the change in attitudes is a subject that merits inquiry. Attention to the problem of "the problem of the aged" may do as much as any other historical examination to eliminate present-day discontents and throw light on issues having to do with understanding and action in the future."[2]

From 1790 to 1864, immediately following the American Revolution to the War Between the States, was a time when the older citizens were given special respect. They were held in high esteem. They were venerated and this veneration became a social norm.

About 1865, Americans' attitude toward the aging started to change. It seems that a new perspective toward the older person was beginning to emerge. This new perspective in some way was affected by medicine. Up to this point in America's history, persons for the most part were taking care of themselves.

As America's culture moved toward the 1900s, medicine began to seek clues for a longer and a more healthy life. Persons became more reliant on doctors' prescriptions rather than old people's advice. That reliance caused problems. Some medical teachers and doctors began to describe old age as an infectious chronic disease, not a normal life process.

Some doctors said that there was no cure for the disease. With experts accepting and teaching these so-called "truths," aged persons began to accept the fact that they did not have any future except to fade away. Along with the scientific factors were the economic influences stressing the myth that the aged person was no longer of any importance in the industrialized society.

During this same period, the youth culture began to emerge. The aging person, because of pressure from a youth-oriented society, began to try to look and act young. Youth was something desired; old age was something endured. Aging persons became captives of a society who was beginning to worship youthfulness.

Most of this attitude evolved out of a man's efforts in medicine, science and industry. A third period in American history was beginning in 1935, the Social Security Act was signed into law. This legislation was a government response to aging as a problem. From 1935 to 1980, the government, at all levels, began to assume a greater responsibility for providing health care and social services for the elderly.

In the early 1980s, possibly the fourth period emerged as there began to be a loud and clear message from the government that it could no longer assume all the responsibility and provide all the funding and programming for our aging population. Their stand was that the elderly have to become more self-reliant and their families will have to assume more responsibility for them.

In this short synopsis of the history of attitudes toward older people, the change is obvious. During the period of biblical times, early church history, Greek and Roman culture, and early American history, the older persons were not a problem to anyone but themselves. Unfortunately, that attitude has changed.

The aged person in America began to be thought of as a problem after 1865. Society in 1935 allowed or encouraged the government to take care of the aging problem. Since 1980 there has been a movement away from the government being totally responsible for the needs of the aging person. At this time it is too early to discuss the ramifications of this apparent departure, or if it will be lasting.

Theologically

Development of an acceptable theology involves some inherent difficulties because religious writers in the field of gerontology have failed to formulate a theological position on aging. However, some theological perspectives can be established.

In the broadest sense, aging refers to the overall process of moving from the time of conception to the end of life. Generally, when people visualize an older person, they conceptualize one who reveals some visible evidence of mental or physical decline.

Even though aging is a process from the beginning to the end of life, society accepts only the last stage as being the whole. When everyone begins to understand aging as a process moving toward completeness, then the transition, which physical impairments or psychological signs evidence will be accepted and dealt with more adequately. More importantly, so will society.

Having not entered the first decade of what many call the last stage of the aging process, I am experiencing the mindset of our society with its myths and stereotypes of aging. It's interesting to note the reaction of friends and others during a discussion of age. For instance, we may be discussing future opportunities in ministry. I state, "My age will not limit my being called as pastor in another church." They reply, "Being in the early thirties will have little, if any, bearing upon opportunities." I reply, "I am now forty-one."

Because of my youthful features and active lifestyle, they have assumed me to be much younger than they are. As they pause to reply to the new information, I can almost see the stereotypes of aging flashing before their minds. They reply limply, "Well, you don't look or act forty-one?" My statement is, "How is one supposed to act at forty-one?" I notice as our conversation continues, they are not quite as insistent that there are as many opportunities for me as asserted before. In ten minutes, right before their eyes, I have aged ten years; and they don't know how to deal with this revelation.

Physically, I feel about the same as I did ten years ago. I hit the baseball farther, although I notice I can't turn the bases as fast during a baseball game. Mentally, I feel great. I think during the past ten years I've done more qualitative learning. Along with other meaningful learning experiences, I finished seminary after thirty-five; and I will finish the doctor of ministry program this year. My memory at times is not as sharp as before. However, maybe I have become more selective because I feel very little memory loss about important things. Chronological age is not the determining fact about what stage of the aging process a person is in. A person who is sixty may reflect age fifty or even forty.

Those who are forty may act and look like they are I the later stages of aging. I am amazed and sometimes shaken as I visit with persons in the hospital or their homes. Everything about them – the physical appearance, the mental attitude, the lack of self-esteem – reflects that they are around the chronological age of fifty. When I ask their ages, they in a resigned voice give the same age as mind or younger. I am shocked. Granted, some, of these persons have had some physical deterioration.

However, the majority of these persons have begun to act and think older than they are – some because they think it's expected, others because they are lonely, depressed or have other reasons. But all have aged before their time. They are speeding the aging process. Thinking old, they act old.

Theologically speaking, unless we are born from above, the aging process has little meaning as it moves to the ultimate ending. Man is born out of a relationship with God. He does not become a sinner; he is a depraved being from the start because of the fall of the original man. When he age of accountability or the age of understanding (whichever one calls it) arrives in the aging process, a person must either accept or reject the son of God as Savior.

When a person accepts God's grace expressed in Christ Jesus, a transformation in life happens. Change in attitudes and lifestyle continue as one lives under His Lordship. Man is thus reclaimed to the state that God created for him and can enjoy the intended relationship with God the Creator. It is this relationship with God during the present age that the true aging process takes place.

Some perspectives in the theology of aging must be accepted if a person is going to enjoy all the aging process he is allowed on planet Earth. I said before that I don't look much older and don't feel much older than ten years ago. But, I am certainly aware that I am older. Certain questions come before me more often.

How much time do I have left to get done all I desire to do? Is my relationship with God as it should be? How about my relationship with my fellow men, my brothers? Are things in order for my family? These are questions people examine and ponder throughout the aging process but which intensify as the last stage is reached.

If people accept the fact in earlier years that they are going to age (most would rather not experience the other option), they would find more enjoyment and fulfillment in the later stages of aging as they ease into them.

The theology of aging has ever-present eschatological overtones. I believe there is not only the present inward spiritual Kingdom of God, but this transcends into the Kingdom of God physical. With this hope in mind, a person can enjoy the aging process regardless of how bad it may seem in later years. God not only rules but will usher in His Kingdom, and each believer will be part of that Kingdom. Eternal life begins in the present. The older life is a stage in the process of becoming all that God intends for man to be.

The 13th chapter of 1 Corinthians will make a good solid base on which to formulate a theology of aging. When a person comes to the last stage of the aging process, the prior years will be far more meaningful if the life cycle has been built upon this truth: "And now these three remain: faith, hope and love, But the greatest of these is love."[3]

W. Harold Mare describes love in a meaningful way:

"Love is the greatest of these three graces; because through faith love unites the Christian personally to God; and through God's love we are enabled to love one another. Love is communicating grace and identifies us as children of God.[4]

"Furthermore, love covers the faults of others rather than delighting in them. It is trusting, optimistic, and willing to endure persecution. In short, it perseveres."[5]

If love, sweet love, that the world needs now would prevail upon the mind of man, aging would be accepted as a beautiful process and not considered a problem in our society.

Faith is acceptance that God is who He says He is. He is the "I am." Faith is the firm belief that *"in all things God works for the good of those who love Him."*[6] During a person's older years, when loneliness attempts to crush, when disillusionment with one's family shatters, when physical pain is excruciating, when mental awareness is clouded, then in faith the aged person can reach out to Father God and know through this sustaining faith that all is well.

Christian hope is more than a person's being hopeful. The believer's hope is on a solid foundation. *"Faith is being sure of what we hope for."*[7] *"Christ in you, the hope of glory."*[8] Christ is our hope. *"For this life we have hope in Christ."*[9] During the aging process we are told to *"be joyful in hope, patience, and affection"*[10] and to have our *"endurance inspired by hope."*[11] The writer of Hebrews tells the believer, *"We have this hope as our anchor."*[12] If a child of God is fortunate to enter the last stage the aging process on this earth, he is assured that he is *"resting on the hope of eternal life."*[13]

F. W. Grosheide, in his commentary on First Corinthians, makes some interesting observations about faith, hope and love in the now and then in verses twelve and thirteen of chapter thirteen.

Commenting on verse twelve he states, "The contrast is one between the "now" and "then", this dispensation and the future, the latter being the period of perfection."[14]

Grosheide continues to point out that in the "then" a believer will know fully. "Even in the realm of glory, as verse thirteen points out, man remains distinct from God. Our knowledge is determined by God's knowledge, which is of the first order. But this much is sure, we shall see things as they are."[15] Grosheide continues describing the same in verse thirteen:

> "Now, not to be taken temporally in this context, but as introducing a conclusion. Paul does not mean to say that faith, hope, and love which abide at this moment, will later on be succeeded by something else, but rather, on the basis of the preceding verses, that they remain for evermore, i.e., not just to our death, or to the end of this earthly dispensation when they will be present at the last judgment, but even to all eternity."[16]

Grosheide gives a more detailed description of faith, hope, and love:

> "Faith in the general sense of the work refers to the relationship between man and God, man and nature. We believe that God is as he reveals Himself. We believe that creatures are as they should appear to be, and although in this dispensation faith is spoiled by sin so that the natural relation between man and his environment is violated. Paul

knows of an antithesis between now and then. Living in the new dispensation we shall experience that we know fully, i.e. that relationship will then be freed from all that is in part. But it remains faith, for even then we shall not know the deep things of God.

"Just as faith indicates the relation between God and the Christian at any given moment, so hope implies that this relation will remain what it is. We hope that all will remain as it is not because we doubt, but because we are certain. The fear inspired by thought of the future is definitely renewed by Christian hope. This hoping is more than knowing, for it involves the whole person and is akin to faith. This hope remains together with faith.

"Love has a somewhat different nature from faith and hope. Love is basic for it does not just refer to a certain relation, but it governs and sustains all relations, because it indicates a direction of life. Love will enable a person to do many things, such as to believe and to hope (verse 5), but it will make it possible for him to hate anything else except sin.

Love is the root of all good actions. Where it manifests itself, and where it must be manifested, it displays a certain quality, i.e., it operates in a certain area. There it adds color to things, it determines the nature and the direction of every action. For that reason it is superior to faith and hope."[17]

Whatever a theology of aging is, it must be expressed in terms which are intertwined with faith, hope, and love.

Acceptance of faith, hope, and love as a foundation for a theology of aging can make the aging process meaningful, even enjoyable. Even though an aged person sees through the window of time dimly, he can be assured there is something better ahead; and it will be permanent.

Sociologically

Aging persons are experiencing changing circumstances within their community. Their lifestyles are being scrutinized under the expectation of their groups and communities. Persons living to an older age are having both indirect and direct impacts on their culture. These rapid changes call for new and more effective study by the social sciences. Changes in the aging process we have thought to be for the better – longer life expectancy, early retirement, and better health – are creating havoc within our sociological systems. In this section we will examine some of these new phenomena.

Most people look forward to retirement. This is particularly true for those who have labored for years at uninteresting jobs or have had to commute a long way to their work. The earlier the retirement the better for many older persons. They have visions of fishing, golfing, traveling, or other chosen ways to spend their retirement years.

But in our highly sophisticated and industrialized society with its developed and accepted work ethic, a person who is not producing has little value. One must produce to be accepted in our culture. How then does culture react to the older person who is not producing according to the accepted norm? Society has tried in different ways to ignore older persons, and therein, reject them.

Older persons learn to expect, accept, and endure different forms of discrimination. In doing so they become enemies to themselves, possibly the worst, because, because they buy what their culture is selling: i.e., they are rejected because they have no productive worth. Societal rejection has other consequences than just the immediate effect on the suffering older person. By rejecting the process of aging in the older stage, the young fail to plan for their later years. Consequently, in the future they are going to be a drain on society's resources.

Not only does society look upon those over sixty-five as being of little productive worth, many of those who retired with high expectation begin to inwardly agree. The dream of all the leisure time to spend in recreation and other activities begins to fade. The elderly need more: they need to be able to again produce in some meaningful way for their self-esteem.

Those who have developed skills in areas other than their chosen or forced vocation find fulfillment. How about those who have no skill in areas other than their prior vocations? There has been an acceptance on the part of some employers to rehire these persons on a par-time basis. Sometimes they will hire two persons to split the same job by the half-day, split week, or every other week. From reports it has been determined that these older workers are as productive as younger employees, possibly more so.

There is volunteer service for the older person who does not need a working income. Volunteer work gives the senior person satisfaction and fulfillment. Some older persons return to school to finish an education interrupted by work. Some attend school just for the pleasure of their learning experience.[18] These persons explode the myth that the older person cannot learn. There are many needs in our society that persons over sixty-five can help meet if society would encourage them to pursue second careers.

There are many isolated and lonely persons in our society over age sixty-five. When older persons are completely disengaged from society, they do not have self-worth and become a burden to society. However, if they participate in some capacity, be it just playing golf, they will be in the production process. From Monday to Friday and even some weekends, mainly in retirement areas, the serious senior golfers flood the golf course. They use clubs, bags carts, riding carts, and balls to pursue their new vocation. They purchase or rent these from the pro shop, golf discount house, or some other house of merchandise.

This vocation produces employment. Where do the retailers get their products? From the manufacturer or wholesaler. And again, this consumption of goods creates employment. We could say the same thing about other recreational activities. The number of recreational vehicles used by senior adults keeps several related manufacturing facilities busy. Without reservation, active senior adults seem to be producers in the fullest sense. Much purchasing power is evident in the senior adult population. Without the buying power of today's older persons, many younger persons would be non-producers.

When Robert Butler wrote his prize-winning book in 1975, a majority of our elderly were below the poverty line. Butler states, "Many, I think most, elderly poor become poor after becoming old."[19] Ten years later, however, an article discussing the annual report of the President's Council of Economic Advisers, recorded the following information about the elderly:

> "Elderly Americans have achieved basic economic parity. With the rest of the population and no longer are a disadvantaged group, according to the President's Council of Economic Advisors. In 1983 the poverty rate for the entire elderly population was 14.1 percent, compared with 15.4 percent for younger Americans, including those under twenty-four, the report said.

"Thirty years ago the elderly were a relatively disadvantaged group in the population, the report said. That is no longer the case. The medium real income of the elderly has more than doubled since 1950. And the income of the elderly has increased faster over the past two decades than the income of the non-elderly population. Today elderly and non-elderly families have about equal levels of income per capita.

"Income levels of the elderly have improved relative to the non-elderly since 1970 because of Social Security benefits increased by forty-six percent in real terms   while earnings from wages and salaries – the major source of income for the non-elderly – decreased by seven percent after adjustment for inflation, the report said."[20]

Sociologically, the onslaught of older persons must be recognized and a constructive program implemented to meet their needs. We are only at the "tip of the iceberg." By the year 2000 and thereafter, the problems and needs will be intensified. Education is needed now beginning with persons aged thirty-five to make them aware of what is ahead and help them to plan for the last stage or stages in the aging process. Basically our culture must do everything within its power to create an environment in which the aging population can obtain and maintain a feeling of self-worth. They will be served and so will society.

Educationally

It seems to be a consensus on the part of most contemporary adult educators that the adult mind is very different from the child's mind. Because of this difference the adults' learning goals and behaviors are extremely different. This means different teaching methodologies. Frequently teachers create a problem by using inappropriate instructional methods for senior adults. Since there is agreement that there is a qualitative difference in the psychology of the senior adult mind, then a **geriogogy** – special methodology for older learners – is necessary.[21]

Andragogy is the art and science of helping the older person learn, as in contrast to pedagogy, the art of and science of teaching children or young persons. It must be kept in mind that even though there is a contrast between the effects coming from both processes.

The following is a summary of a comparative analysis of the two processes discussed by Meyer: Pedagogy assumes that there is a captive audience consisting of younger learners who are there to receive knowledge. The teacher has arbitrarily decided upon the content with the concern in mind to prepare the learner for the future. The important agenda is that the learner absorb certain knowledge so that more complex knowledge can be learned. There is little regard for how the individual learner feels about what is being taught. The curriculum guidelines and teachers decide what is to be learned.

Andragogy, in contrast, assumes an interest of the older adult learner must be stimulated before participation in course work becomes a reality. In this process the adult learner is viewed as entering any course with a wide background of prior learning and experience which can be utilized from mutual input to define a condition in which the teacher is basically a guide who also benefits from the older learner's input.

The learner has input both in the content and how it will be taught so that this active involvement leads not only to enhance self-concept but also to increase knowledge, both consequences leading to the mutual betterment of the participants. Problem solving and principles are important. And one's feeling about course content is viewed as a basis for retention.[22]

> "In short, pedagogy assumes that a student is moving through the process of learning phenomena toward maturation, at which point andragogy enters the picture and assumes that the learner has already arrived. Androgogy is based on the assumption that older learners are more concerned with solutions or approaches to immediate, rather than to long range problems; they enter a learning experience with wide, diversified histories, therefore, having a particular set to learn; and they are, in general, independent and self-directed."[23]

There is at the present a realization that learning and relearning are life-long tasks, calling for continuing education through all the years. This is of utmost importance in those years of later maturity when individuals must make considerable, sometimes difficult, changes in practically every aspect of their living habits.

Society has not yet fully recognized that the growth processes from infancy through old age involve a succession of transitions. People give up what they have, with some difficulty, learned to replace it with some new pattern of thinking or activity.

They must find ways to identify themselves with their developing capacities so they can cope with their enlarging human relations as growing individuals. Consequently, people, many times, must unlearn – relinquish – what they have previously learned and master something new. In order for them to accomplish this new learning, they must keep more or less flexible, and retain their abilities for entering into new relations and developing new techniques.[24]

Senior adults operate within a social order. This social order is not an impersonal system located in outer space and operated by indifferent agencies. Social order is the relationship of all the persons who make up the group and is maintained by their beliefs and actions:

> "Social order is in people, and social change and development occur essentially in the minds and hearts of people who not only make those choices and decisions that direct social change, but who also translate those choices and preferences into their own individual actions and varied relationships.
>
> "Here we see that the dynamics of social life and of social change arrives from the beliefs and expectations, the hopes and the fears, and by their purposive strivings, maintain a social order that reciprocally governs their way of life. A recognition of this dynamic circular relationship of the individual gives increased significance to the need for adult education and especially education for later maturity. Indeed, it is the only way in which we can hope to maintain a self-regulating free society."[25]

Education for the aged is a new challenge that must have a degree of emphasis on relearning or what some may call unlearning. The process of education for senior adults must undertake to help persons become aware of their assumptions and preconceptions, enabling them to look at these critically, then to deliberately revise or replace these assumptions in light of new knowledge, understanding, and insights:

> "Education for later maturity may thus be viewed as an occasion for continued self-discovery and new learning, formerly organized for those who seek that kind of experience, but in any event leading to new interests and activities and genuinely creative endeavor. This becomes peculiarly appropriate and possible in later maturity, since, often for the first time since childhood, the older person has freedom from pressing responsibility and leisure to reflect, explore, and create in various fields an endeavor."[26]

It should be understood that senior adults come to any educational experience with backgrounds that vastly differ from those of a child, adolescent or younger adult. The latter are, for the most part, concerned with their preparation for specific goals and are willing to accept the requirements and guidelines of their teacher.

Senior adults generally do not come with the same need or with the same pressures. Therefore, they are usually not ready or willing to fall into a prescribed pattern. Senior adults have long accumulated life experiences, many curiosities and perplexities. They may have aspirations that are not clear in their own minds but which they wish to pursue in their own ways and at their own tempos.

Most of the time the older learner will respond to the educational process and enter into the group discussions only when these have a meaning for them as individuals:

> "We live primarily by memories and expectations. The older person, whose expectations are progressively curtailed, turns in his reveries and reflections increasingly to his past. He lives over again his triumphs and defeats, preoccupied with the effort to understand himself and how he became what he is. The programs of discussion groups for the older person may serve primarily to provide new and more fruitful leads for the individual's private reflections, offering more promising ways of interpreting his past experience and developing more self-acceptance."[27]

It is important that the educational program for senior adults involve their voluntary participation in the planning and administration. They will then feel that they are being treated with dignity and respect for their abilities, interests, and years.

The teacher of senior adults must be careful not to embarrass the students during the learning process. The teacher, through planning, should minimize the chances for the senior learners to make mistakes so they will desire to continue toward success. It would be well for the teacher to become acquainted with information about each of the senior learners. Many times the difficulty the senior learners have are self-imposed; some may feel they cannot learn new things:

> "Planning for adult learning involves planning for situations so that the learner gets a sense of mastery and success. Mastery may come from showing the individual that he can learn, or by showing the aspects of the task that he can do already. Teachers of the adults must appreciate that the adult brings with him a past – a past of experiences

with attitudes which may be capital to work with, or a deficit to be overcome. Using the capital or clearing the deficit may be the basis for the complete sense of satisfaction that teaching gives the teacher and that learning gives the learner."[28]

One thing that a teacher of senior adults should be prepared for is that older individuals, on average, will tend to learn more slowly than youth. They will also need some help to compensate for their lesser vision and hearing. To overcome some of these problems, the teacher should talk more loudly, more clearly, and more deliberately; also it is wise to reiterate important points.

There should be good light in the room, and a room temperature should be maintained that will keep the seniors comfortable. The teacher should be able to be seen by all the students. The blackboard or preferably an overhead projector, because of its larger print projections, should be used for new names and strange expressions. This gives additional strength to the spoken messages.

The teacher should plan class sessions with not more than a fifty-minute time period and be sure there is enough of a break so there is time to use the facilities. It is important to allow time for feedback through questions and the sharing of individual experiences. This gives the senior opportunity to integrate the new learning with pas experiences.

Also, the teacher needs to adapt to the students in the class. A class is never made up of persons who are exactly alike but rather consists of persons who differ in experience, capacity, intent, and skills. The teacher should attempt to determine the means or general level of attainment within the group and gear the teaching accordingly. In general, it is best to teach on a senior high school level. Even though some of the seniors may not have finished or even begun high school, their life experiences should enable them to participate at this level.

I learned some years ago as a Bible instructor that the best learning took place when a person participated by doing. We were taught to teach first by telling, then showing, and then doing. Doing is always better than passively accepting.

This is certainly true with senior adults – get them doing. Get them participating, even if only through questions and discussion. Learning is encouraged to continue when learners can recognize visible results. There needs to be some method where the learners can recognize positive results. This can be done with a simple pretest and post-test containing the same questions.

The greater number of sensory avenues to which material is presented, the more likely is there learning and retention. It is well to combine audio-visual materials with discussion and action. In conclusion, there is no doubt that senior adults can experience meaningful learning. They need proper motivation in subjects that they have an interest in.

Chapter 2
Endnotes

1.   Rolf P. Knierim, "Age and Aging in the Old Testament," in *Ministry with the Aging*, ed. William M. Clements (New Y ork: Harper & Row, 1981), p. 35.
2.   Martin E. Marty, "Cultural Antecedents to Contemporary American Attitudes Toward Aging," in

Aging," in *Ministry With the Aging*, ed. William M. Clements (New York: Harper & Row, 1981), pp. 56-67.

3. 1 Corinthians 13:13.

4. Frank E. Gaebelein, gen. ed., *The Expositor's Bible Commentary*, 12 vols. (Grand Rapids: Zondervan Publishing House, 1976), vol. 10: *1 Corinthians*, by W. Harold Mare, p. 270.

5. Ibid., p. 268.

6. Romans 8:28.

7. Hebrews 11:1.

8. Colossians 1:22.

9. 1 Corinthians 1:22.

10. Romans 12:12

11. 1 Thessalonians 1:3.

12. Hebrews 6:19.

13. Titus 1:2.

14. F. W. Grosheide, "The First Epistle to the Corinthians," in *The New International Commentary on the New Testament*, ed. F. F. Bruce (Grand Rapids: W. B. Eerdman's Publishing Company, 1953), p. 311.

15. Ibid., p. 312.

16. Ibid.

17. Ibid., pp. 313-314.

18. *Aging America: Trends and Projection* (Report from U. A. Special Committee on Aging, 1983), p. 89.

19. Robert N. Butler, *Why Survive? Being Old in America* (New York: Harper & Row, 1975), p. 26.

20. President's Council of Economic Advisors Annual Report, 1983, quoted in *Greensboro News and Record*, 3 January 1985.

21. Carroll B. Freeman, *The Senior Adult Years*, (Nashville: Broadman Press, 1979), p. 61.

22. S. L. Meyer, "Andragogy and the Aging Adult Learner," *Educational Gerontology.* An International Quarterly, vol. 2, (April 1977), pp. 115-122.

23. Victor M. Agruso, *Learning in the Later Years*, (New York: Academic Press, 1978), p. 128.

24. Wilma T. Donahue, *Education for Later Maturity* (New York: Whiteside, Inc., 1955), p. 5.

25. Ibid., p. 6.

26. Ibid., p. 12.

27. Ibid., p. 14.

28. Ibid., p. 57.

Chapter 3
Aging

Demographics

In the first chapter of this book some demographics were discussed in an abbreviated way. Now a more detailed examination is needed:

> "There are at present about 27.4 million persons age sixty-vive and older in America. Among those, women consist of 59.9 percent and men 40.1 percent, white persons over sixty-five are 90.5 percent, black 8.1 percent, and others 1.4 percent."[1]

Other interesting findings by the Census Bureau and reported in September 1983 are:

> "Those eighty five and older – the fastest growing group – will make up five percent of the U.S. population by 2050, up from the slightly more than one percent today.
>
> "The number of people sixty-five and older increased twice as fast as the rest of the population between 1960 and 1980.
>
> "The elderly black population grew faster than did that of the elderly whites, reflecting a significant narrowing of racial differences in life expectancy.

> "Among old people, women now outnumber men by three to two – a big change from the five to four ratio of 1960.
>
> "Social Security benefits go to 91.2 percent of the aged and are almost the total income of one out of five.
>
> "Sixty-nine percent of Americans sixty-five to seventy-four voted in the 1980 elections. Their participation rates second only to the fifty-five to sixty-four age group."[2]

This same report by the Census Bureau killed some stereotypes. About eight of ten elderly persons described their health as good or excellent when asked to compare their health with others of their own age. Furthermore, only five percent live in nursing homes; two-thirds of all homes owned free and clear belong to elderly persons.[3]

By using the same rate of increase from 1982 to 1983, one can project a number of 28 million plus Americans over sixty-five years of age at the conclusion of 1994. This represents eleven to twelve percent of the total population. In the year 1990, there were approximately 32 million older Americans. This was 12.7 percent of the total population.[4]

In 1900 the median age was about twenty-three; 1940; twenty-nine; in 1980, thirty. It is projected that in the year 2000 the median age will be approximately the age of 40.[5] Many workers in the field of aging are already saying that aging should not begin at sixty-five but at a much later age.

Summarizing these figures and other related information should give us some insight into needed adjustment for our planning. Not only is our individual planning affected, but also is the church ministry where the average church member will be living five to ten years longer. New knowledge about life expectancy, for instance, challenges churches to prepare that young girl in

Sunday School who is going to live to be ninety years of age. What is going to be done to help her live a full life and be a viable resource in her family, community, and church?

Understanding Terms In Aging

A definition of terms is needed before further discussion of aging. First, gerontology is the study of the normality of aging. When the word aging is used rather than aged, this gives emphasis to a process over time. Many people, as they approach gerontology, see aging only as a study at a certain point in time. In gerontology there is an emphasis on process.[6]

Some gerontologists in the past have looked on the senior person as they age as a social problem; but if they are consistent with the definition of gerontology, they will give emphasis to the normality of aging. If one can accept that aging is normal, it will be understood that aging can be an asset, an adventure, a potential, a resource to understand, incorporate, and utilize in the ministry of the church. Having said this, it is not overlooked that as one ages there are losses. But at the same time, there are gains.

A term sometimes expressed in a place of gerontology is geriatrics. Geriatrics is a study or a science of the relationship of disease to aging. Geriatrics is a very narrow field in the overall field of gerontology, and the two concepts should not be confused.[7]

A term which should be of special interest to pastors and others working with the aging person in geriophobia – a fear of aging.[8] Some of the difficulties people have in ministry to the elderly is that they have difficulties with their own aging. Unless the church professionals are able to deal in a satisfactory way with their own aging, they will not be successful I their work with the elderly. There are barriers created when people who minister see something in the person to whom they are ministering that is disliked or feared. Church professionals must recognize their individual phobias and examine the scriptures in order to arm themselves with a philosophy and theology which help them overcome their phobias. Many of these phobias are formed early in life because of the misconceptions of what an aged person is like.

Two terms previously used also need to be clarified. The life span was described as being he maximum years a human can live; life expectancy is the anticipated years a human will live. Most statistics used in the project deal with life expectancy.

Stereotypes, Myths, Ageism

As mentioned in an early chapter, many of the problems of the aged are attributed to their acceptance of stereotypes, and myths about aging. What is a stereotype? Stereo types are a common tendency to characterize a group of people without regard to individual differences. There are many variables in life and what stereotyping allows a person to do is to categorize, to organize.

Consequently, there is a functional or important value for stereotyping and a good reason for its continuance; there's always some truth in stereotypes. Positive stereotypes are still just as wrong as negative stereotypes, but people have benefited from them. Examine the stereotype that most older people are poor. Have older people benefited because of this stereotype? Yes, by senior citizens' discounts and tremendous growth in Social Security benefits, among other ways.

Even though there are some positive stereotypes, most rest on the negative side. Stereotypes can be hurtful; stereotypes can be inappropriate; they can be harmful. To say that elderly people are rigid, unable to change, and will not change is untrue. An illustration would be the adjustment a person makes after the death of a spouse. Also, older persons in the present fast-moving technological society are having to make changes all the time.

It is said older persons are not creative , are not active – they are passive. We only have to look at some of the great artists, writers of this day, and outstanding political leaders to get some understanding of the potential of later life. When a person begins to see an older person in some described dysfunctional way, then the stereotype becomes negative.

In this writer's church are several capable senior adults. But when they are asked to perform a task, they say they are too old. They have convinced themselves of this fact because of the stereotypes they have listened to for years. This is, perhaps, the greatest tragedy about stereotyping that society has created, i.e., the aged person buys the stereotype. For the good of the church and society, these stereotypes must be destroyed.

When these stereotypes become accepted by the majority of society and become norms, another force is created to be reckoned with: ageism. Robert Butler coined the word ageism and defines it:[9]

> "Ageism can be seen as a process of systematic stereotyping of an discrimination against people because they are old, just as racism and sexism accomplish this with skin color and gender."[10]

Robert Butler, in discussing ageism as he does, expresses that he believes our society has a profound prejudice against later life. Why? It probably has something to do with death and one's own mortality. Being around older persons reminds person unconsciously of where he is headed himself. Although ageism is expressed in subtle ways, older persons realize they do not have the value in society they once had. Ageism has strong negative effects.

There is also institutional ageism. The institution of health care is an example. Unfortunately, some doctors treat older patients with less concern than others. Possibly this goes back to some doctors' attitudes around the turn of the century. Possibly these attitudes are changing. How about the church? Is it an institution? How much importance has it attached to quality ministry with senior adults? Does it give them as much ministry as it gives others in the church?

In addition to the negative effects of stereotyping, myths, too, have a negative effect. Ageism is perpetuated by myths. A myth is a notion based more on tradition or convenience than fact. In the second chapter was a presentation of how chronological age is misunderstood and how all persons over sixty-five are generally placed in the same category.

Another myth is that of stagnation. Later life is not a time of stagnation but of change, as was noted before. There are always challenges ahead.

Robert Butler suggests that age brings with it a disposition for certain things in life. First, humans desire to leave a legacy:

> "Human beings have a need to leave something of themselves behind when they die. This legacy may be children and grandchildren, work or art, personal possessions, memories in the minds of others, even bodies or part of them for use in medical training and research.

Motivations for the tendency toward legacy are generally a combination of not wanting to be forgotten, of wanting to give oneself magnificently to those who survive, of wishing to remain in control in some way even after death (for example, through wills), of desiring to tidy up responsibility before death. Legacy provides a sense of continuity, giving the older person a feeling of being able to participate even after death."[11]

Second, Butler talks about the elder function:

"Closely connected with legacy, the "elder" function refers to the natural propensity of the old to share with the young the accumulated knowledge and experience they have collected. If unhampered and indeed encouraged, this "elder" function takes the form of counseling, guiding, and sponsoring those who are younger.

It is tied to the development of the interconnectedness between the generations. It is important to a sense of self-esteem to be acknowledged by the young as an elder, to have one's life experience seem as interesting and valuable; on the other hand, it can be devastating to be shrugged off by seemingly uninterested younger people as old fashioned and irrelevant.

Not all older people, however, have a **nurturant feeling** toward the young. Some, because of their life experiences, look upon the young with envy and distrust.

"Mental health personnel can learn much about how to help older people by respecting and benefiting from what he elderly have to teach. This occurs through listening to them with an open mind, reading the writings of older people, viewing their arts, hearing their music, and in general absorbing the culture created by them."[12]

The third thing that Butler discusses is the older person's attachment to familiar objects:

> "An increasing emotional investment in the things surrounding their daily lives – homes, pets, familiar objects, heirlooms, keepsakes, photo albums, scrapbooks, old letters – may be noticed. Such objects provide a sense of continuity, aid the memory, and provide comfort, security and satisfaction. Fear of loss of possessions at death is a frequent preoccupation. Older people generally feel better if they can decide in an orderly manner how their belongings will be distributed and cared for. Younger family members or friends should take concerns seriously, offering their help rather than denying that the older person will someday die. Possessions may have to be painfully given up before death as a result of moves from a house to an apartment, an institution, and so on. Some institution are now recognizing the value of encouraging people to bring some of their own familiar possessions with them."[13]

Then the last thing Butler suggests is the change in a sense of time:

> "There are may be a resolution of fears about time running out, with an end to time, panics and to boredom, and the development of a more appropriate valuation of time. While

the middle aged begin to be concerned with the number of years they have left to live, older persons tend to experience a sense of immediacy, of here and now, of living in the moment. This could be called a sense of "presentness" or elementality." The elemental things of life – children, plants, nature, human touching, physically and emotionally, color, shape – assume greater significance as people sort out the more important from the less important. Old age can be a time of emotional and sensory awareness and enjoyment.[14]

Butler's arguments quite clearly reveal that a person does not stagnate developmentally or intellectually. It is true that people suffer decline in intelligence as they grow older. It could, perhaps, be said that there are two kinds of intelligence: fluid intelligence and crystallized intelligence. This concept comes from some lecture heard in the past. Fluid intelligence involves that ability we have to solve problems and this ability does not decrease in later life.

People in later life are not as good or as quick at solving problems as they once were. Crystallized intelligence, on the other hand, involves accumulating knowledge and that ability increases with age. This concept depicted on a graph would show one aspect of intelligence declining but the other aspect of intelligence increasing.

With these thoughts clarified, the myth about declining intelligence in later life can be exploded. When a statement is made about declining intelligence, one needs to ask what kind of intelligence a person is referring to. So much for the myth of stagnation. In older years, a person does change and a person does increase in crystallized intelligence.

The next myth that needs to be explored is abandonment, that there are many elderly persons who are ignored by their families. Many family members of older persons are receiving unwarranted criticisms in regard to the issues of abandonment.

Persons within the total family structure do not live in one big house as they did in earlier American history. However, research of most communities across this land will reveal that family members live close enough to each other to maintain contact. Those who move to other areas for retirement chose to leave their family for various reasons.

The caregivers within the family situation, usually women, are giving much of their time taking care of a parent or relative. Certainly there are cases where the family does abandon the older persons, but this situation is not the norm. families do continue to be involved with their older members.

Churches need to be constantly aware of the fact that their membership is not ignoring their older members or dumping them in nursing homes, unless absolutely necessary. These members, in regard to their family, do not need to be told what they ought to do. In most cases they are doing "the ought to." What they need is information about how they can do "the ought to" more effectively. In all areas of family life, churches are big on advice about what a person ought to do without providing information about the "how to."[15]

Another myth that requires special attention is senility. This is a destructive term; it's a hurtful term. The term "senility" doesn't tell anything about a person. Often people will go to the doctor after experiencing a little memory loss. They can't remember as they think they should, or they are confused. They are diagnosed as being senile when they may have a significant brain syndrome taking place in their lives. They are given an aspirin and sent home. (These physiological impairments will be discussed in the section on biological aging.) The myth of senility is very destructive, and one should be very careful in using the term, if it is ever used.

The myth that many older persons are in institutions also needs to be dispelled. Possibly church members and ministers are more aware of this problem because of the time involved in nursing homes, rest homes, old age homes, and county homes. When the names of persons institutionalized are published in a bulletin or church newsletter, persons may think that a large percentage of the older members are there. As discussed in chapter three under demographics, only five percent of persons over age sixty-five are in nursing homes. However, if one considers the number that enter and leave nursing homes over a period of time, the figure would average about ten to fifteen percent.

Sometimes community care is stressed too much. The nursing home decision is difficult to make. Sometimes it is an appropriate decision. However, if some family members push too hard for a nursing home or other institutional care, they do a great disservice not only to the older person but to the caregiver. One needs to be aware then of the myths surrounding older persons in institutions.

After looking at some of the widely accepted myths and stereotypes that led to ageism, what implications can be observed for the church? Just being the church presents a marvelous and wonderful opportunity to deal with ageism. The starting of one's feeling of ageism involves many factors; one is the sociological experience. Our children are taught ageism. How can the church counter that? The main way is to get older adults involved again. Activities should be planned between senior adults and younger persons. In this writer's church, most of the children's classes or departments attempts to provide older adults as teachers or helpers. Children can then be with and touch an older person. They can experience an older person, and we can in the church begin to deal with ageism in that way.

Another way ageism can be destroyed is to create an environment of acceptance within the church. If a senior adult does not feel at home within the church. If a senior adult does not feel at home within the church family, there must be corrective measures taken.

The church must do whatever is required in senior adult ministry to bring about a sense of acceptance to the older person. It is not only to the group, but to individuals that a stand against ageism needs to be taken. The church should allow older persons to express that they are there and that they have ways to be a resource in the church.

Creative ministry would allow those kinds of opportunities. The church must take into account when programming not only that there are age differences within the membership, but that there exists within the senior adults great age differences. The church must distinguish between the young old and the very old. Older persons must be given an opportunity to express their needs within the church family.

In conclusion, it is important to stress that the koinonia must be what be what Christ intended it to be: a caring fellowship creating caring relationships. The church must maintain a fellowship where the Spirit of God can come in and affect the membership so that when older persons enter, they know they are accepted; they know there is caring fellowship. This attitude partially fulfills Christ's command *"Unto the least of these my brethren."* That is the bottom line. The church members have a tremendous opportunity to deal with the stereotypes and the myths in ageism. Through an understanding of the aging process and with capable leadership, the church can have a powerful impact on the rest of society.

Chapter 3
Endnotes

1. Pictogram, "Spotlight on Older Americans," *U. S. News and World Report*, 2 July 1984, p. 53.
2. "Census' Latest Count of Older Americans," *U. S. News and World Report*, 10 October 1983, p. 8.
3. Ibid.
4. *Aging America*, p. 5.
5. *Greensboro News and Record*, Quoting U. S. Census Bureau, 21 June 1984.
6. Robert N. Butler and Myrna I. Lewis, *Aging & Mental Health*, (New York: New American Library, 183), p. 368.
7. Ibid.
8. Ibid.
9. There seem to be two ways of spelling ageism: ageism or agism. Robert Butler was the first person to give the word description. Frank Stagg spells the word ageism throughout the book, The Bible Speaks on Aging, (Nashville: Broadman Press, 1981).
10. Robert Butler, *Why Survive? Being Old in America*, (New York: Harper & Row, 1975), p. 12.
11. Butler, *Aging & Mental Health*, p. 11.
12. Ibid., p.12.
13. Ibid., p. 13.

14. Ibid, p. 14.
15. Ibid, pp. 129-133.

Chapter 4
Elderly Concerns

This chapter will discuss in an abbreviated fashion four areas of concern for the aging person. There is some overlapping in these topics. The subjects to be discusses are economics of aging, living arrangements for the elderly, legal aspects, and community resources.

Economics Of Aging

What is the economic status of the elderly? Even though the elderly are better off today than a few decades ago, still the economic condition of the older person is generally "at a lower level and is much less secure than that of the younger population."[1] "In 1981, three-fourths of the elderly had incomes below $10,000 compared with forty-two percent of those aged twenty-five to sixty-five years."[2] Some of the elderly are very rich. A lot have adequate income. A larger number have a very modest income – close to poverty. The significant minority experiences poverty based on the poverty index as defined by the government:

> "Lower incomes in the elderly population are associated with factors over which elderly persons themselves have little control: their sex and race, the health and survival of their spouses, and their own health and ability to continue work at acceptable wages. Older people who work full time tend to have income similar to younger persons of

the same race and sex. For many elderly who do not work, Social Security payments are vital."[3]

The inflationary period of the seventies wiped out the cushion that many persons were depending on for retirement. Money that had been put away for the retirement years was spent on increased costs of utilities and higher food costs. Even though the income levels are low compared to those of the younger adult population, the latest round of inflation has not affected the older person as much as the younger population. The real median income of the elderly remained about constant from 1980 to 1981.

The median income dropped a few percent for the younger population during the same period.[4] "Using constant 1981 dollars, the median income of the elderly person has increased substantially every decade since 1951."[5] The number of elderly persons below poverty level is 14.6 percent.[6]

The way the government figures the poverty level index seems very simple. The United States Department of Agriculture decides what a person needs in food to maintain an adequate diet.

That amount is then multiplied by three. Persons above that amount are alright. Are they? Think of the plight of the elderly without the Social Security programs and other governmental programs – both those services received automatically and those received on a need basis.

While attending the seminar it was discovered that:

"Social Security benefits are the single largest source of money for the elderly. These benefits reach 91.2 percent of the elderly population. Over half of this group depend on Social Security for over half of their income, and a fifth receive ninety percent or more of their income from this source."[7]

At its conception, Social Security was never intended to be more than a support system for other types of retirement income. Down through the years people have begun to depend upon Social Security as their total retirement package. This is a mistake. In our society people cannot exist very well on just Social Security income:

> "More than 65 million Americans, 30 percent of the 224.3 million people living in non-farm households in this country – received direct benefits from the federal government. So discloses a new U.S. Census Bureau study, 'SURVEY OF INCOME AND PROGRAM PARTICIPATION.'
>
> "It reveals that 31.7 million persons are getting Social Security payments, and 26.7 million are receiving Medicare aid. These are the two most common benefits. The study reveals further than almost twenty percent of the entire population is receiving some financial help based on its low income status. This percentage includes those who receive food stamps, Medicaid, subsidized housing, aid to families with dependent children, and similar benefits."[8]

Just what is Social Security?

> "Retirement survivors and disability insured benefits are paid under a social insurance program administered by the Social Security Administration, a Federal agency. A person must file an application for benefits, and he or she must meet certain eligibility requirements. The payments made under this program are commonly known as 'Social Security benefits.' They are paid monthly."[9]

The money that people receive from Social Security is money that they or other persons have paid in over the years. The program of Social Security was intended to be essentially self-financed out of payroll taxes paid by the worker or employer.

The media frequently point out that in the 1940s, forty-five to fifty persons were paying for one Social Security recipient. It was projected that before the 1990s expire, this rate will be down to two paying and one receiving. This ration is even with a higher percentage of payroll taxes on increased earnings.

The bailout of the past few years may not be good enough to keep the Social Security system in strong financial condition. One important question is evident: how long are thirty-year old workers going to be willing to pay the large annual Social Security tax bite and the same time not feel any assurance that there will be something when they retire?

There are signs of rebellion on the part of the young professional now. In the 1970s retirees received their total investment in about eighteen months.

In addition to Social Security, there is Supplemental Security Income (S.S.I.), a federal program administered by the Social Security Administration. It pays people in financial need who are sixty-five or older or who are blind or disabled. Only one percent of all money that is spent by the government on the elderly is designated to S.S.I., however.

In addition, the Medicare and Medicaid programs provide fifty billion dollars in benefits to the aging person. This is about twenty-five percent – twenty-two percent Medicare, three percent Medicaid – of total dollars spent by the government on the elderly. Medicare is a federal program of insurance and money from trust funds which pays hospital and medical bills for entitled people. Medicare benefits are generally paid on a beneficiary's behalf to the person or organization that furnished the health care service. It pays covered inpatient hospital costs except for four hundred dollars on each benefit period.

Medicaid is an assistance program which is funded by money from the Federal, State and local taxes and pays medical bills for eligible persons. Medicaid is a Federal-State partnership. States designed their own Medicaid programs within Federal guidelines.

In 1982, between twenty-five and thirty percent of the total federal budget was spent on programs directly helping the elderly. The breakdown of the total spent by the government on programs for older persons is as follows: fifty-seven percent on Social Security, twenty-two percent on Medicare, three percent on Medicaid, one percent on S.S.I., two percent on veterans' retirement, two percent on housing, and three percent on other programs concerning the elderly.[10]

Living Arrangements For The Elderly

What do older persons do about living arrangements when they retire? Most continue to live in the same place. Some move to a warmer climate. Some may move to where their children live, since the children's work prevents them from being close to their parents. The University of Florida Professor Stephen M. Golant studied independent elderly persons and found that they are generally happy persons:

> "Over eighty percent of the elderly nationwide live in ordinary homes and apartments in ordinary neighborhoods. Over ninety percent reported that they were generally happy with their lives.
>
> "Eighty percent had lived in the same home more than five years, and fifty-seven percent said they definitely would not move; only nine-percent definitely would like to relocate."[11]

After studying the results of his survey, which includes much more information than cited, Golant continues:

> "If we understand better how they cope with old age, we may be able to help more people to remain in their own homes, living independently."[12]

There comes a time in the lives of many older persons that they lose their ability to live independently. What are some signs that they are unable to cope on their own? Dr. Stanley Cath, psychiatrist and medical director of the Family Advisory and Treatment Center, Belmont, Massachusetts, described these signs:

> "Obviously, in addition to memory loss, cognitive decline, losing their way, emotional outbursts, there are severe physical handicaps such as a progressive immobilizing arthritis, prolonged paralysis from strokes and hearing or visual loss. Frequently, especially in widows or widowers, there are emotional, financial, geographical, and social considerations. With the death of a

spouse, there may be a re-appearance in many older people of the terrors of childhood, especially the fear of being alone. A lot of, otherwise, perfectly competent human beings in their seventies or eighties suddenly develop this panic. They seem unable to remember things or care for themselves simply because of terror. But this is a treatable condition."[13]

Persons with these signs are able to stay in their homes with the proper support service or help from key caregivers. They need human contact; this is vital. These persons may come to a time that it is too dangerous for them to remain on their own.

If their home or apartment is scrutinized, there will be signs that reveal that the problem needs immediate attention. These signs consist of spoiled food in their refrigerator or no food, burnt towels near the stove, repeated falls, unattended bedsores, and inability to recognize friends or even immediate family members.

When it becomes undesirable or impossible for aging parents to live by themselves, one alternative, for them is to live with one of the children. Many middle-aged children would like to bring their parents into their homes and care for the parents now as they cared for their children. However, there are some major factors that children should consider before having an aged parent move in with them:

"They must consider their tolerance for a three-generation household and ask: Can the woman of the house get along with the particular aged parent? Despite modern changes in the women's roles, ninety percent of the time women are the ones who will care for the aging generation. In some cases, can they stand a mother or a father waking up in the middle of the night terrified, making a mess at the table, or telling grandchildren stories about the parents as children?"[14]

Other items that need to be considered include: Is the spouse agreeable? Would the noise of children or the activities of teenagers create insurmountable problems? Is there the proper amount of space? Can the correct amount of care be provided by family members? If the older person does move in, there should be some understanding between all parties in advance.

Of most importance is the authority question. It's not easy for the parent to give up authority. What will the procedure be when conflict develops between grandparents and grandchildren? There should be rules regarding small things like the use of television and bathrooms.

The three-generational family living together can be a meaningful relationship if it is characterized by love and respect. If the relationship between the parents or one of the parents, and either one of the adult children is distant or in conflict, it can be a difficult time, however.

When the option of the aging person moving in with the children is ruled out, there is the choice of a nursing home. Regardless of what many may think, this is not an option desired by many of the children.

Only five percent of elderly persons are in a nursing home at one time. Sometimes because of space in the children's homes, finances, family commitment, and usually the main one, the necessity for skilled nursing care, a nursing home becomes necessary.

How can a nursing home be rated as a good one? Persons who have a relative there should be consulted. The food and housekeeping should be checked. The social and psychological atmosphere should be accessed along with the quality of nursing and medical service. Will the home allow the aged persons their personal doctor to care for them, or does the house physician care for all the patients?

Residents' dress and cleanliness should be observed. Is the staff warm, sensitive, and cheerful? Do the staff and residents seem to be in warm communication? Social workers who know about the home should be questioned. What percentage of nursing homes could be described as happy, safe, comfortable places?

> "I'd say about eighty percent. Like most, it is a respectable but perfect industry. We have the best nursing homes in the world, but many have problems. Many lack good staff."[15]

When a nursing home is being considered, the person going there must be allowed as much input as possible. If it can be arranged, they should visit the homes under consideration.

After the aged person is in the nursing home, they shouldn't be allowed to feel abandoned or discarded or as some writers say, "dumped." The visits of family members or friends are the most important resource for the person in the nursing home.

The younger members should be prepared for the distinct odor that lingers in most nursing homes. By seeing the whole family on some of the visits, older members will feel part of family life. They need their family and want to spend some time with them.

Many times the family member who had to make the decision to place the elderly member in the nursing home will feel guilty. This should be discussed with a trusted friend or a pastor. Either can help in working through the grief process.

Legal Aspects

During the class session on legal aspects a local attorney discussed the making of wills, executors, and ways to give the power of attorney. There were many questions asked by the aging participants, and the attorney answered the questions, seemingly, to their satisfaction.

One thing which the attorney omitted in this session that was discussed with the class participants at a later date was the living will. Most of the class members had never heard of the living will. Many states now recognize the rights of individuals to have a will dealing with only their desires as related to terminal illness.

Larry Richards' book contains a typical form designed to deal with possible legal questions raised by the failure to use life-prolonging means.[16]

> To any and all doctors, hospitals, health personnel, and others treating me during my illness:
>
> I, _____, hereby make this statement in the presence of witnesses, to declare and record my expressed wish and desire that: In the event, due to illness or accident, that my condition becomes terminal and without reasonable hope of recovery, then I do not wish to be kept alive by the use of drugs, treatments, or machine. I wish to receive adequate medication for proper control of my symptoms, but nothing beyond what is necessary for that purpose. I, hereby, specifically withdraw my consent for any such primary life

sustaining treatment, and this withdraw of my consent shall continue unless and until I revoke it in writing. Should I, in the course of my illness, subsequently become legally incompetent or unable to communicate my wishes to those treating me, then this document should be considered as continuing to withdraw my consent to any further treatment not directed primarily at symptom relief.

Any and all doctors, nurses, hospitals and institutions that honor my wishes and intentions as expressed in this document, are, hereby, formerly held free from any and all liability on behalf of myself, my heirs, successors and assigns.

(Signed)_____

(Date)_____

(Witness)_____

(Witness)_____

Community Resources

During the community resources sessions a representative from the local social service agency shared with the group different services that are available within the community. Interest was keen and many questions were asked.

Our community, population two-hundred thousand, has most of the resources found in the larger metropolitan areas. Our community has bus transportation to pick up older persons at their door so they can be taken to doctors, pharmacies, or the grocery stores. There are food centers at different locations for a hot lunch at minimal or no cost. There are many senior activity centers.

Chapter 4
Endnotes

1. *Aging America: Trends and Projection* (Report from U.S. Special Committee on Aging, 1984), p. 26.
2. Ibid.
3. Ibid.
4. Ibid., p. 29.
5. Ibid.
6. Ibid., p. 38.
7. Ibid., p. 33.
8. *Parade Magazine*, 2 December 1984, p. 16.
9. Ibid.
10. *Aging America: Trends and Projection* (Report from U. S. Special Committee on Aging, 1984), p. 40.
11. *St. Petersburg Time*, 18 November, 1984.
12. Ibid.
13. *"If You have to Care for Your Aging Parent,"* U. S. News & World Report, 3 October 1983, p. 75.
14. Ibid., p. 76.

15. Ibid.

16. Larry Richards and Paul Johnson, *Death & the Caring Community* (Portland: Multnormal Press, 1980), p. 41.

Chapter 5
Psychological Aspects of Aging

Psychology as related to the field of aging could be a complete project within itself. The following discussion will briefly cover the mental disorders of old age with emphasis on the two disorders which are of most importance to older persons: depression and organic syndrome.

Mental Disorders Of The Elderly

"The mental disorders of the elderly have generally been divided into two kinds: the organic disorders, which have a known physical cause, and the functional disorders, for which at present no physical cause has been found and from which the origins appear to be emotional – related to the personality and life experiences of people. The division between organic and functional disorders is breaking down, however. Social and psychological factors have been identified in the "organic" disorders and spectacular advances in the neurosciences reveal biochemical (physical) correlations with "functional" disorders.[1]

"The extent of mental disorders in old age is considerable. It has been estimated by the American Psychological Association that at least three million or fifteen percent of the older population need mental health service."[2]

Butler goes on to say that he would consider that number a conservative estimate. Many older persons have chronic physical illnesses which also have associated reactions requiring attention. Older persons tend to underreport their mental illness, and many do not seek help.[3]

There are two groups of mental patients: those who were admitted to hospitals at an early age and grew up there and those who have developed mental illness later in life:[4]

> "Assessment of the older persons' impaired function is critical…Diagnosis and treatment as well as prevention, must go beyond their traditional psychiatric diagnostic evaluation to include the context in which symptoms develop and the healthy assets and resources of the personality.
>
> "We would warn against a rigid preoccupation with obtaining a 'correct' diagnosis. The diagnosis should be flexible and open to testing through careful, sensitive observation of the older person. If a particular treatment direction is not working, everyone involved should back up, rethink the issue and begin again in a new direction. Above all, the diagnostic past is to establish the basis for a functional, workable, useful treatment – just as much emphasis should be on determining what is remedial as in simply establishing what is wrong."[5]

Functional Disorders

For many years mental disorders in old age were thought to be related to brain damage. This notion has proven not to be true. It is true, however, that the incidence of mental illness does increase with age. It is difficult to always clearly define "functional" or "organic" disorders:

> "Functional disorders such as depression may have biochemical causes or accomplishments and patients with "organic "disorders may have lifestyle and other psychosocial determinates and consequences."
[6]

A listing of functional disorders will include: psychosis, schizophrenic disorders, paranoid disorders, neurotic disorders, paranoid disorders, neurotic disorders, affective disorders, bipolar disorders, major depression (unipolar) and other depression, anxiety disorders, somatoform disorders, dissociative disorders, psychosexual disorders, and personality disorders. (A detailed description of each of these disorders and their relationship to the older person can be found in Butler and Lewis, *Aging & Mental Health*, pp. 58-74.)

Depression will be discussed in some detail in the last part of this chapter, but before leaving functional disorders we need to examine what Butler says about suicide:

> "The highest rate of suicide occurs in white men in their eighties. Suicide is one of the ten leading causes of death in the United States. Older persons, about eleven percent of the population, account for roughly twenty-five percent of reported suicides – about five thousand to eight thousand yearly – in 1970, and this is still roughly true today."[7]

Butler goes on to discuss the fact that in addition to the usual methods of killing themselves by not eating, by not taking medicines, by drinking too much, by delaying treatment, or by taking risks physically. He believes that with proper treatment the suicides related to depression would be prevented.

Organic Brain Disorders

The general characteristic organic mental disorders found in older persons are described by Butler and Lewis:

> "The term `organic brain syndrome' now refers to a constellation of psychological or behavioral signs and symptoms (for example, delirium or dementia) without reference to causes. `Organic' mental disorder means a particular organic brain syndrome in which the cause is known or presumed (for example, multi-infarct dementia). The `organic brain syndrome' is more general term while `organic mental disorder' is more specific."[8]

To put it more simply, `organic brain syndrome' is a group of symptoms which develop because of damage to brain tissue."[9]

Impairment of memory: In this sign, recent memory is affected by damage to brain tissue function. The older memory traces seem to be deeper and more intact while things that have happened recently are not associated with those earlier memories. Possibly this memory pattern may be due largely to a lack of alertness and attributed to the damaged organ, the brain.[10]

Impairment of intellect: This can be an intellectual loss which is shown in the inability to do mathematical calculations. Because such mathematical calculations require a fairly recent memory, there seems to be some correlation between memory, there seems to be some correlation between intellectual and memory losses.[11]

Impairment of judgment: Individuals who have lost their judgment may not be able to make proper decisions in regard to finances, business dealings, and so forth.[12]

Impairment of orientation: This sign appears when people generally do not know others around them. Sometimes they do not know where they are. They do not even have the knowledge of the hour, the day, the year, or knowledge of current situations.[13]

Liability and shallowness of affect: In this mental sign there is a rapid mood swing. The changes may be dramatic and instantaneous.[14]

The damage of brain tissue affects a person in some areas of physical and psychological function. In many cases organic brain syndrome can be reversed. For example, Butler states in another book:

> "The failure to diagnose and treat reversible brain syndromes is so unnecessary and yet so widespread that I would caution families of older persons to question doctors involved in care about this."[15]

Butler adds that reversible brain syndromes are characterized by various changing levels of awareness rather than a fixed disorientation:

"Hallucinations may be present, usually of the visual rather than auditory type. The patient is typically disoriented, mistaking one person for another, and other intellectual functions can be impaired. Restlessness, usual aggressiveness, or a dazed expression may be noticed.[16]

"The two most common organic brain syndromes found in older people are delirium and dementia. Both syndromes imply relatively generalized cognitive impairment. Delirium is most often seen in the very young or old (after sixty), while dementia is predominantly seen in the old or less commonly in those approaching old age.

"The syndromes overlap and may represent different phases of widespread brain pathology. Delirium is currently viewed as an acute brain failure resulting from widespread derangement of cerebral metabolism and neurotransmission disturbance. Dementia is viewed as a result of pathological changes in cerebral neurons or their death."[17]

A few direct quotes from Butler and Lewis's book give a brief synopsis of delirium:

"Delirium usually develops over a short period of time from hours to days...Delirium may evolve slowly, especially if it results from systematic illness or metabolic imbalance. The term 'reversible' is a more useful description; reversibility of the clinical course, even if not the cause of the brain pathology, remains the one consistent characteristic, especially if the diagnosis and treatment are applied promptly and accurately. Delirium in its most subtle forms remains a frequently undiagnosed illness, more so in the United States than in some other countries, for example, England.

"A sign of delirium is a fluctuating level of awareness, which may vary from mild confusion all the way to stupor or active delirium. Hallucinations may be present, particularly of visual rather than auditory type. The person typically is disoriented mistaking one person for another, and other intellectual functions can also be impaired. Speech may be incoherent and thinking is disordered. Remote as well as well as recent memory is lost. Behaviorally, restlessness, a dazed expression, or aggressiveness may show themselves. And the person can appear frightened either by disorientation or as a result of the vivid visual hallucinations. Delusions of persecution may be present. It is important to note that there are no consistent or characteristic neurological findings in delirium except for the presence of abnormal movements like various forms of tremors.

"Delirium has a relatively brief duration, usually less than a week. One consequence of failure to identify and treat delirium is death from an underlying and undiagnosed cause; another is that the disorder may shift to a more stable organic brain syndrome, and the older person then becomes a chronic patient, often in a long term institutional care facility or nursing home."[18]

Butler and Lewis make the point that dementia brain syndrome is no longer thought to be irreversible.[19] If there is true senility, it occurs when organic brain syndrome has become irreversible.[20]

Butler refers to two major conditions that create the mental disorders often termed "senility." One is cerebral arteriosclerosis (hardening of the arteries of the brain); the other, unfortunately referred to a senile brain disease, is due to a mysterious dissolution of brain cells."[21]

Alzheimer's Disease

Alzeimer's Disease is the frequently seen type of presenile dementia.[22] The brain appears to waste away. "In the earlier stages Alzheimer's Disease can be mistaken for behavioral disorder and also may be complicated by emotional reaction to the organic changes.[23]

Alzheimer's Disease then is caused by an accelerated loss of brain cells. According to the experts humans are all born with more brain cells than they need. They usually begin losing them at an early age. But this loss does not affect the ability to think, work, or carry out day-to-day responsibilities.

Alzheimer's Disease s a subject that's appearing in special segments on television and discussed on the talk shows. This disease is tragic for the person who experiences it, but there are also many far- reaching consequences for the family, particularly those who are the caregivers. In many cases, the church can do very little for the person experiencing the disease, but members can be supportive and helpful to the caregivers. Almost all caregivers experience great frustration because of their lack of understanding of Alzheimer's Disease.

This frustration gives way to depression in some cases. They feel trapped and experience anger. The emotional involvement of these caregivers is beyond most pesons' comprehension. Regardless, caring persons from the church can perform ministry by being available to listen and perform needful tasks for the caregivers during their trying times. Many more characteristics, causes, and symptoms could be discussed about organic brain syndrome, but this should be enough to give some awareness of the subject.

Depression

What is depression? Archibald D. Hart identifies depression as the following:

> "Depression is the most complicated of our emotions and yet one of the most common of psychological problems that a person can experience. Probably one of every five people will experience it seriously enough that it will hinder their normal way of life. Basically it is a feeling of gloom or sadness which is usually accompanied by slowing down of the body. Depression is just not in the head but is experienced throughout your whole body. It's in your stomach as much as in your head."

> "Depression can be seen as three things: as a symptom, a disease, and a reaction. As a symptom, depression is part of the warning system of the body calling attention to something being wrong. It accompanies a wide variety of physical disorders such as influenza and cancer, and certain disturbances of our endocrine system also gives rise to the symptom of depression. In its severest form, the psychotic depression is a disease – an illness category all of its own. Finally, depression is a reaction to what is going on in life and more specifically, to significant losses in life. These depressions are the kind that most people contend with in their daily life."[24]

Gary Collins comments that:

"Depressions can occur at any age (including infancy), and they come in various types. Reactive depression (sometimes called exogenous depression), for example, comes in a reaction in some real or imagined loss or other life trauma. Endogenous depression seems to arise spontaneously from within and usually is found in the elderly. Psychotic depression involves intense despair and self-destructive attitudes, often accompanied by hallucinations and loss of contact with reality. Neurotic depression is mixed with high levels of anxiety. Some depressions are chronic – long lasting and resistant to treatment. Others are acute – intense but of short duration and often self-correcting. Many professionals would distinguish all of these from discouragement, which is a mild, usually temporary and almost universal mood swing which comes in response to disappointments, failures and losses.

"All this implies that depression is a common but complicated condition, difficult to define, hard to describe with accuracy and not easy to treat.[25]

Freeman, in his discussion on depression, says he likes to look for the "D's" as disillusionment, disappointment, despair, discouragement, doubt, diminished, self-esteem, and desolation. Freeman goes on to say that accompanying the psychological attitudes and feelings revealed in the list of "D's" are the basic physical signs of depression, such as loss of weight, sleep, appetite, energy, and the problem of constipation.[26]

After evaluating what has been written by four different writers about depression, it seems that depression appears to be a disorder of moods and feelings. A symptom is the nerves. "Nerves" refers to the psychomotor response of the body to the emotional condition. In our society persons will speak about a case of "nerves."

This week a local church member is in the hospital in fluctuating state of depression. She talks about her nerves. Her hands and body tremble. She had had degrees of heart failure in the past.

The bottom line is that she admits to being afraid of death and is unable to cope with that fear. When she is alone and begins to think about dying, the trembling starts and sometimes she becomes so nervous she can't breathe. She has been under professional care, and I've talked wither, but nothing seems to bring her out of a depressed mood for a prolonged period. She is a Christian; she prays, but she can't let go of her fear or fears.

The whole idea of "nerves" isn't very specific. What we are really talking about is nerves being something in the body itself. We say that thoughts are in the head and feelings are always in the body. The depression that a person has is always in the body some place. One of the main helps that a resource person can give to older persons is to help them understand what their center of depression is.

Another symptom of depression has to do with appetite. Persons, if they are depressed, may eat more than they normally do. Some have learned that food is a comforting thing; so when they are emotionally upset or distraught, they eat, or they may hardly eat at all. The key is the significant change from the normal. The feelings a person is expressing are a symptom of depression. It may include the feeling of worthlessness, excessive guilt, and self-depreciation – the putting down of oneself.

Fatigue is generally associated with depression in older persons. They claim they don't have the "get up and go" they used to have. There is also a loss of interest in life. Older persons will say nothing interests them anymore, nothing gives them pleasure. Often the sex drive is decreased or disappears in depressed state. They say, "I don't have interest any longer in sexual activity."

The last symptom to be discussed has to do with a change in sleep patterns. A person complains of too much sleep or too little sleep. Like appetite, a change in the sleep pattern is an important thing to notice. Sometimes depression will cause distressed sleep or no sleep during a period one expects to sleep.

If an older person is having significant difficulty with two or three of these symptoms, there is a possibility that the person may be suffering from a period of depression. Depression is treatable. If depression is recognized, the physician can prescribe medication. Medication can help in breaking the destructive cycle of depression. Then with the right therapy, an older person can get out of the depression.

Church ministry persons need to be aware of the signs of depression among senior adults and try to help; and if the depression continues to deepen, the helpers should suggest professional guidance for the depressed persons.

Chapter 5
Endnotes

1. Robert N. Butler and Myrna I. Lewis, *Aging & Mental Health* (New York: New American Library, 1983), p. 55.
2. Ibid.

3. Ibid.
4. Ibid., p. 57.
5. Ibid., p. 58.
6. Ibid., p. 59.
7. Ibid., p. 72
8. Ibid., p. 75.
9. Carroll B. Freeman, *The Senior Adult Years* (Nashville: Broadman Press, 1979), p. 170.
10. Butler, *Aging & Mental Health*, p. 76.
11. Ibid.
12. Ibid.
13. Ibid.
14. Ibid.
15. Robert N. Butler, *Why Survive?* (New York: Harper & Row, 1975), pp. 175-176.
16. Ibid.
17. Butler, *Aging & Mental Health*, p. 77.
18. Ibid., p. 78.
19. Ibid.
20. Freeman, *The Senior Adult Years*, p. 172.
21. Butler, *Why Survive?*, p. 10.
22. Butler, *Aging & Mental Health*, p. 88.
23. Ibid.
24. Archibald D. Hart, *Depression: Coping and Caring* (Arcadia: Cope Publications, 1981), pp. 4-5.
25. Gary r. Collins, *Christian Counseling* (Waco: Word Books, 1980), p. 85.
26. Freeman, *The Senior Adult Years*, p. 176.

Chapter 6
Biological Aging

There's a difference in the true age of a person and the age that can be attributed to a person because of deteriorative changes that have taken place. Many of these changes would never have taken place if proper prevention had been maintained. A person can prevent almost all of the "aging" changes or at least delay them.

Basically there are three things people need to do if they want to protect themselves from most of the changes that come with aging: eat right, exercise right, and sleep right. In addition they should use proper care to protect their skin and avoid the use of certain things – mainly tobacco and alcohol.

Adhering just to these simple rules will make all the difference to the person throughout the aging process. These good habits should be maintained in all the stages of life, and the sooner they started the better. Persons can start at the later stage in life – sixty-five and over – and improve their daily life and life expectancy. The old adage "use it or lose it" is true, and all should adhere to it.

If adults can maintain a youthful appearance, they generally will feel young. If they allow themselves to begin looking old, they will feel old.

In saying all this, there is no intention of trying to influence adults not to accept their chronological age or to revert to a youth-culture mentality. However, chronological age is overemphasized in how one is supposed to feel. Just because I am forty-two is no sign I am supposed to feel and act like some others I know who are forty-two. Of course, some of these persons have had physical deterioration because they have neglected the good habits we have mentioned. But others look old because they think it's expected of them to look old.

Persons in past generations spent much time working outside, especially exposed to the sun and other elements – which generally caused them to appear older than they were.

Consequently, some persons have pictures in their minds of a past generation when they visualize an older person. That's the way they think they should personally look. If they think this long enough, if they project this picture in their mind long enough, they will begin to look and act like the caricature they have visualized.

Biological Aging Of The Body Systems

This writer's thoughts will be interspersed with those from chapters two and three in a book by Jane Ogle, *Ageproofing*. This book gives an excellent overview of the important body systems and their component parts as related to aging. For the most part, the way she writes about each of the subjects can be understood by the non-professional. She discusses the changes that tend to occur in the average person and asks an important question of each: "Is it a true biological aging process and, therefore, inevitable?" She has determined that many things thought to be just a part of true aging are really the result of abuse, avoidable disuse, and chronic diseases.

Dermal System

The skin is generally subject to long abuse and results in wrinkling, blotchiness, sagging, and other signs of so-called aging. This is not true biological aging process. Skins need to be protected from the sun, wind, or cold. These all bring injurious results and consequently, the aged look. Skin that is protected and taken care of will look the same until the person's latest years.

Older persons may notice that they do not sweat as much as they have in the past. This becomes noticeable between the ages of forty to sixty. However, through exercising often and strenuously, the sweat glands will begin producing again.

In our society hair gets more attention than skin. An aging person loses it or it turns a new color. By age forty a number of persons are gray. In older years, in many cases, hair will turn white. Baldness affects all white men to some degree because of the decrease in density of the hair as they age:

> "But, whereas in non-balding scalp hair density may drop from, say, about 700 hairs per square centimeter at age twenty to about 500 at age fifty, with only a slight further reduction in density during the years following, the density count goes much lower in a balding scalp, falling to about 350 hairs per square centimeter between ages fifty-five and seventy and down to about 275 between ages seventy and eight-five."[2]

In contrast to the hair loss as one ages, there is also an excessive growth of hair, particularly in women who have passed through the menopause. So in some persons, no hair, and others, more hair.

Nails also go through changes as age increases. Younger persons will have about fifty percent more growth of their fingernails than those persons sixty-five.[3] Men's nails usually grow faster than women's until about fifty.

Then men's nails grow about the same until age seventy, while the women's nails grow faster. I've heard my wife remark that her nails are brittle and break easily. "They didn't use to do that." This brittleness may last for four years possibly due to hormonal changes at the menopause.[4]

Musculoskeletal System

If people's bones become porous, weak, and fracture- prone, health can become affected. Some persons accept that this is going to happen. This does not necessarily need to happen. Even in later years, bone deterioration can be reversed through proper diet and exercise.

The muscles begin to deteriorate after persons reach their peak strength (age for men twenty to thirty, women by age twenty). Little loss occurs before age thirty-five to forty. But by the time a man is sixty, he will lose ten to twenty percent of his maximum strength, and a woman will lose even more. Again, a program of rigorous exercise will prevent the decline of muscle and reverse the loss, regardless of age.[5] For example, my wife and I bought an Exercise One for each other. In just two months use, both of us can feel the difference in our muscle tone.

Joints are found where two or more bones have some kind of connective tissue. There is little known about how or to what extent a joint ages. But much of the joint deterioration blamed on aging clearly has to do with disuse, abuse, or chronic disease.[6] For instance, in a few moments after writing for two or three hours, I will get up from my desk. My joints will feel stiff. Think of what happens if a person doesn't exercise over a period of time.

Persons are reconciled to the myth that they will lose their teeth if they live long enough. Not true. Teeth can be kept a lifetime if they are properly taken care of. Abuse is the reason that a large percentage of our population experiences tooth decay.

Cardiovascular System

Providing oxygen without which a person would die, is the job of the cardiovascular system:

> "What are the age-related changes in cardiac function that do matter? They involve three main factors affecting oxygen delivery. One is the output of the heart. Another is the blood's capacity to transport oxygen to the tissues. And the third is the ability of the tissues to extract the oxygen they need from the circulating blood. The output of the heart is a product of the heart rate or number of beats a minute and the amount of the blood propelled out with each beat...The maximum heart rate at any given age is roughly estimated by subtracting a person's age from 220.
>
> "The key thing to keep in mind is that the heart is a muscle. The lower maximum heart rate in an older person may be due to increased stiffness of the heart's muscular wall...Until quite recently, most experts in exercise physiology believed that the effects of age on heart muscle were inevitable and irreversible. Now direct evidence from human performance laboratories is starting to show the tendency of the heart to stiffen and take longer to contract can be countered by regular, vigorous exercise of sufficient duration."[7]

Respiratory System

The oxygen supply is good and the heart is working efficiently, but as one gets older the lung efficiency must be taken into account also.

"Certain anatomical changes that may occur with time do have deteriorative effects on the lungs. The rib cage may become more rigid – its cartilage may show signs of calcifying, and the joints about which the ribs rotate may stiffen. The respiratory muscles may get weaker, particularly if a person has a sedentary lifestyle. Degenerative changes may be seen in the vast network of alveola, the capillary-laced outpouchings at the furthest ends of the bronchial tree through which gas exchange between lungs and blood takes place. Some capillaries atrophy. And the elastic fibers, so vital in maintaining the resiliency of the lungs' airways, tend to decline in both thickness and number.

"Is a decline in vital capacity inevitable? Little, if any, seems to occur among people who keep fit and healthy and do not smoke.

"Exercise can increase vital capacity in healthy young men and women and reverse losses that have occurred in older ones. Tests with the latter have yielded some spectacular results. As much as forty years of accumulative loss was cancelled out by a conditioning program. A six-week stint brought a five percent gain and after a year the gain went up to twenty percent."[8]

Gastrointestinal System

The gastrointestinal tract consists of the esophagus, stomach, small intestine, colon, liver, pancreas, and gallbladder. Again, if a person eats properly, excercises regularly, and gets enough sleep, there shouldn't be any drastic change due to the biological aging process.

Renal System

"The kidneys increase in weight from birth to about age thirty, after which a reverse process gets under way. By age eighty, an accumulative decline of twenty to thirty percent has usually occurred. The marked drop in weight is due to the loss of close to a third of certain key components in each kidney's one million filtering units, or nephrons. There is a corresponding drop in the filtration rate of substances reaching both kidneys from the bloodstream and also a decrease in the renal blood flow.

"Just how inevitable is all of this? New research indicates that the kidney deterioration is due not to aging as much but rather to excessive protein in the diet...Bringing the diet more in line with what people are naturally adapted to through evolution can do a great deal to prevent kidney decline."[9]

Reproductive System

The period of time that a woman goes through menopause can be very distressing:

> "The changes that lead up to, accompanying, and following the menopause are, of course, far more obvious than those which older men may experience. They are genetically programmed and part of the true aging process. They cannot be prevented, delayed or reversed by any known natural means. And the fact that the menopause occurs at a relatively early age, often well before fifty, compounds its potential traumatic impact."[10]

Men feeling a sense of decreased potency in later life can experience depressed feelings:

> "Older men who keep in good physical shape can apparently maintain their output of sex hormones at the level of young men.
> "Men in their seventies and eighties who are sexually active have stepped-up levels of testosterone; they show no drop whatever in concentrations of the hormone as a result of age. They ejaculate as many sperm as twenty-year olds, the one difference being that the proportion of immature sperms seems to increase with advancing years. In spite of this, male fertility can continue into extreme old age. Men in their nineties have fathered children."[11]

Immune System

When a person grows older, the immune system as the front line of defense tends to become less efficient. "The immune system is responsible for the body's self-defense, protecting every organ, tissue, and cell against danger from without or within."[12] When a person exercises, the circulation of white blood counts increases:

> "From a basal level of 5,000 to 8,000 per cubic millimeter of blood, they soar to as many as 35,000 after a quarter-mile spring lasting only a minute. The greater the amount of exercise stressed, the more the white blood cells multiply."[13]

The white blood cells are the front line of defense against disease. Recent study of cells have revealed that red blood attack body invaders as well as white cells. "The red blood cells are also the primary agents for carrying away what remains of enemy forces after each onslaught, in this way preventing any potentially harmful caches from being deposited in susceptible areas."[14]

Nervous System

"The nervous system, with the brain at its center, governs the workings of every cell, tissue, and organ in your body, guided by the ceaseless flow of information it receives and processes from without and within the various senses. What happens to this immeasurable complex intelligence and control system over the years is obviously of crucial importance to you.

> "The brain itself undergoes certain changes over the years. The most obvious one is loss of weight. After reaching a maximum between twenty-vie and thirty-five, weigh slowly decreases until by eighty or eighty-five it has dropped by ten to twenty percent. Neuron,

or nerve cell atrophy accounts for most of the reduction, which is not uniform.

"Not only are neuron losses selective in region and timing, but smaller nerve cells are eliminated in greater number than larger ones, the smaller cells being younger and at an early stage of development. Nerve cells follow the rule, `Last in, first out.'

"A spectacular new technique shows vividly that brain activity levels do not decline with the years. Using radioactive tracers, it measures how much glucose is being metabolized and where, and produces a color-keyed chart displaying the results – a sort of cerebral weather map. Readings disclose that glucose utilization, and therefore brain activity, rises during a person's growing years and then remains constant throughout life.

"What this means, actually, is that the metabolism of each neuron is higher in an older person's brain than in the younger one's and that the older brain simply has to work a bit harder in order to maintain the same level of functioning as the younger one.

"If you keep our brain in the best possible shape from day to day – with the conditioning that vigorous physical as well as mental activity provides – it remains primed for stressful levels of activity. Physical activity and mental activity enhance each other's effects."[15]

In early mid-life and after, there seem to be all kinds of changes taking place in the visual system:

"The most important change that occurs in the visual system as people get older has to do with the transmission and reception of light.

In order to stimulate light, a certain optimal range of light must reach and be absorbed by the photoreceptor, or light-receiving, cells of the retina at the back of the eye.

"The pupil plays a very significant role in light transmissions because it controls by its constant dilation and contractions, the amount of light admitted into the eye.

"The pupil is not the only part of the eye that undergoes changes affecting light transmissions. There are more extensive ones in the lens.

"By age sixty only a third as much light may reach the retina as in age twenty, and the retina itself may become less efficient. The result is a loss of acuity – the ability to distinguish fine detail – and of image resolution.

"As people in America grow older, their ability to hear well also declines...The quantitative change is due to the loss of elasticity in the part of the auditory system known as the middle ear. The eardrum may thicken and stiffen. And the ligaments connecting the minute bones of the middle ear to one another may become less flexible, thus muffling vibrations transmitted to the shell-shaped organ of the inner ear called the cochlea. Such conditions usually reflect a poor blood supply resulting from heart disease, high blood pressure, or other cardiovascular disturbances. They are not to be blamed on aging as such.

"The qualitative impairment comes from irreversible damages to the inner ear, specifically, the cochlea, with its vulnerable little sound-sensing hairs. Especially marked is the loss of sensitivity to higher frequencies. But here again, there is no reason to believe that the damage is due to inherent aging processes as is commonly thought. Most often it is the result of prolonged exposure to loud noise.

"'Old hearing' hearing results not from getting old but rather from a lifetime of abusive exposure to noise, together with subtle effects of chronic degenerative disease – all things that you can do a great deal to preven."[16]

This synopsis of some of the biological systems of the body should promote an understanding for those working in the field of ministry to the aging.

Impotence

The subject of impotence requires the attention of the church professional. He needs to be able to understand men who are experiencing frustration with this problem. This is a subject that cannot be taught in a mixed-class group or even discussed too successfully in just a class of all men, even though they did discuss it in full detail on television – 20/20.

Too often, even in this day, the family doctor will lightly pass over this problem if confronted by a patient – "it's just in your head." They, so many times, look at it as just a psychological problem.

Many psychiatrists, psychologists, medical doctors, and urologists are finding it to be more of a biological problem than thought over the past years. Of more importance biologically, there is help through surgical techniques. A search for a Christian book containing some information on the subject of impotence revealed nothing more than a cursory treatment of impotence.

Chapter 6
Endnotes

1. Jane Ogle, Ageproofing (New York: Nal Books, 1984), p. 8.
2. Ibid., p. 14.
3. Ibid., p.15.
4. Ibid., p. 16.
5. Ibid., p. 18.
6. Ibid., p. 20.
7. Ibid., p. 23.
8. Ibid., pp. 25-26.
9. Ibid., p. 28.
10. Ibid., p. 29.
11. Ibid., p. 31.
12. Ibid., 31.
13. Ibid., p. 33.
14. Ibid., p. 34.
15. Ibid., pp. 36-38.
16. Ibid., pp. 39-40.

Chapter 7
Coming of Age

Senior adults need the retirement benefits they began and worked for; they need to feel needed and wanted – not cast away. As I researched this topic I can see the aging beginning to move into a position of acceptability with our society. We need to get the older participants feeling personally related to what was happening overall to aging in our society.

Aging Has Come Of Age

Aging in America certainly has come of age popularly. This does not mean that persons desire to come of age or be older. Look at the topics of conversation. A person engaged in conversation with another over a period of time will discuss the age of someone or the age of something. Aging has become a popular subject for the media.

National news magazines have complete stories on aging. More and more about aging is appearing on television as a special or as a segment of a special. There is certainly no end of the writing of books on aging.

Another reason for the popularity of aging is America's acceptance of leisure. This is not leisure in the sense that some would think of leisure, but leisure in the sense that people choose their activities and have more control over how they use their time.

Aging has also been a political concern for a long time. Those who are in office recognize the total number of older persons out there. They recognize the propensity of those older persons to vote. The sixty-five to seventy-five age group went to the polls during the 1980 election in greater numbers than any other group except fifty-five to sixty-five.[1] Politicians, many times, bow to the pressure brought upon them by senior adult organizations.

The greatest characteristic assigned to aging and older persons is that they are problems. Younger persons have a great concern that the elderly are a burden. Younger persons are concerned about the impact on them as their parents grow older. Economically, they are perceived as a problem. Socially, older persons are considered a problem because their social activities have to be provided. Housing also must be furnished. Health wise aging persons are a problem because more dollars have to be provided to meet the needs of their failing health.

It should be noted that these are preconceived needs; these are preconceived problems – problems, yes, but preconceived in a greater degree than older persons themselves perceive them to be.[2] Although the problems are not as great as viewed by society, the aging person is observed as problem by many.

One way or the other, aging affects any person who is alive. They, the aged, are parents; they are our neighbors; they are fellow church members; they are our fellow countrymen. As a result, there is a great concern for the aging person personally.

Youth and middle aged persons begin to recognize the time is coming when they will be a member of the aged group. There was a time when a person could say, "But I will not live that long."

In this present time, one cannot say that. Not all are going to live "that long," but according to statistics, a great majority will. Aging has come of age personally. It is not something to be pushed aside, winked at, passed over in conversation, or ignored in the media. Aging is something very, very personal to each person.

Life expectancy is moving upward for those who are born today and in the tomorrow's. Life expectancy for those persons who come to their middle years is increasing tremendously. Those persons can look forward to number of years of quality life. This concerns many personally.

Reactions To Coming of Age

Reactions to the fact that aging has "come of age" are very evident in our community responses. "Community" means the cities, towns, countries, and states, and volunteer agencies. All of these are responsible to some degree for programs, senior centers, community centers, informational and referral centers, housing, food and clothing, transportation, educational opportunities, and leisure opportunities for the older person. Communities and organizations are responding to the needs of the aging person throughout this country.

Responses to this "coming of age" are also seen in the federal government. Congress has enacted a number of laws to provide for meeting the needs of older persons.

Churches have also responded to the needs of older persons. In fact, throughout church history, the church has responded to meeting the needs of older persons. Many denominations have special offices or departments and special programs for meeting the needs of the older person.

Local churches have responded to the needs of older persons in various ways. The early senior centers were mostly established by churches. The church's home visitation program, such as Meals on Wheels, has been picked up, carried on, or subsidized by the government.

What are the demands for the church pertaining to aging's "coming of age"? What does "coming of age" require of the church? Many things can be suggested, but there are two considered very important. One is to obtain knowledge about the process of aging. That's the purpose of this present project. A person needs to understand the aging process. Adults need to understand their own aging.

Jesus said, *"I have come that they may have life and have it to the full."*[3] The second important demand for the church is that it must be determined under the leadership of the Holy Spirit to become a caring fellowship in which a senior adult may find the full life and grow in the full life.

Chapter 7
Endnotes

1. Aging America: Trends and Projection (Report from U.S. Special Committee on Aging, 1984), p.83.
2. Ibid., p.79.
3. John 10:10.

Chapter 8
Biblical Perspectives On Aging

The Bible does not discuss the aging process in any detail. It would be difficult to use the Bible to proof-text many things happening today in the aging process, but it does give many perspectives about aging. Rolf Knierim says that there are 250 passages in the Old Testament concerned with old age.[1]

Biblical Perspectives For Understanding Aging

Some biblical perspectives for understanding aging need to be discussed. What principles, what perspectives can be found in the Bible to help one understand the whole aging process?

Aging is in God's plan for His creation. "There is a time for everything and a season for every activity under heaven; a time to be born, a time to die."[2] The Bible recognized the totality of life being God's plan.

It is also God's plan that there should be progression to man's life: "*The length of our days is seventy years – or eighty, if we have the strength; yet, their span is but travail and sorrow for they quickly pass, and we fly away.*"[3] In these verses the scriptures seem to be saying that according to God's plan, there is length in life. Also, if people take care of themselves and develop strength, the years of their lives could be increased.

There is a quick look at the life cycle in Jeremiah, when the writer speaks of the wrath of God being vented: *"Pour out on the children in the street and on the young men gathered together; both husband and wife be caught in it, and the old, those weighed down with years."*[4] These verses clearly indicate that the Bible shows stages in life and that these stages are part of God's plan.

After Solomon is told he is to become king, he pleases God by telling Him that he needs help; he asks for wisdom and understanding. God tells Solomon that since he has not asked for wealth and long life, he will receive riches and great honor.

He will also receive a wise and discerning heart – the wisest man ever. In addition to all this, he will have a long life – this last is a conditional promise. *"And if you walk in my ways and obey my statutes and commands as David your father did, I will give you a long life."*[5] Solomon did not obey. Solomon did not have a long life. The reward of a long life was missed because of disobedience.

In Genesis, God assures Abraham that he and Sarah are going to have a son. God also makes another promise to Abraham at this time. *"You, however, will go to your fathers in peace and be buried at a good old age."*[6] Again old age is a reward for being obedient to God.

From a biblical perspective, wisdom and understanding come with aging. This wisdom does not necessarily come to all the aged because some persons do not appropriate for themselves that which is available to them as they age.

Job says, " Is not wisdom found among the aged? Does not every life bring forth understanding?"[7] Elihu, in speaking to Job, demonstrates there is wisdom among the young. There is understanding in youth. But there is a quality of understanding and a quality of wisdom which only comes with the aging process.

The Bible teaches that older persons can still contribute to society. This is quite contrary to modern day thinking. Moses needed help. The people were grumbling and griping.

They were not satisfied with manna from the Lord; they preferred the garlic and onions of Egypt. They were wailing at the entrance of Moses' tent. He cried out to God for help. And the Lord provided it, possibly from an unexpected source. The Lord said to Moses, *"Bring me seventy of Israel's elders who are known to you as leaders and officials among the people...They will help you carry the burden of the people so that you will not have to carry it alone."*[8]

God would use these older persons to help Moses accomplish His purpose. God still has tasks for seniors today. God's Spirit rests upon them (today within them) as it did the elders of that day to enable them to serve. There is retirement today. There was retirement in biblical days. However, there is no retirement from obedience to God in whatever service He desires of the senior adult. There is a need in the church today for the continuing service of senior adults.

To get the true perspective of the aging process, one needs to recognize that there are some negative things that happen during the aging process. The Bible speaks of being old and losing strength.[9] Reference is made to the fact that as a person ages, the eyesight grows dim.[10] This was not true of Moses because we read that his eyes were not weak.[11]

Even though rare, some very old persons today need no eyeglasses to read. David asks the aged Barzillai to come to Jerusalem with him so David would take care of him. Barzillai's answer reveals that he was eighty years old, had no taste, and impaired hearing; his sensory functions were operating in a weakened state.[12]

This same weakness abides today. But through modern technical aids, improved eyesight and hearing in all ages is possible. These are natural process that happen in some way to most aged persons. They slow an older person somewhat, but they shouldn't stop the elderly from functioning in a useful way.

Personal Bible Perspectives

If a person is going to be able to deal with the aging process involving members of society, then he must deal first with his own cycle of aging. The Bible speaks to the individual about what he must do if he is to experience successful aging.

To age successfully, a person must fear God. *"The fear of the Lord adds strength to Life. But the years of the wicked are cut short."*[13] The beginning of becoming and achieving that which God provides is an acceptance of His love sacrificed on the cross – His Son Christ Jesus. He becomes our Savior and our Lord.

To become the persons that God wants individuals to be, they must accept the total of life as a reality. Joshua had served God and Israel well as a young man and throughout his life cycle. As he was approaching death, he called the leadership of Israel together and without any apology said, *"I am older and well advanced in years."*[14] Joshua, like all people, had one other option beside growing old.

Frank Stagg writes about accepting the total life:

"Aging does not just become a problem in old age; for some there is more trauma in turning thirty or forty than in turning sixty or seventy. Many children want to be older than they are, and many adults want to be younger than they are. Some people go through life wanting to be older until they switch to wanting to be younger, never knowing the joy of being what they are. This identity crisis is a proper concern for the young and the old, not just for the elderly. A daily column poses the question, 'Why Grow Old?' The obvious answer is that the alternative is to die young. The question implies that 'old' is bad, a dogma which needs to be examined. Aging should be on the side of maturity, wisdom, goodness, and fulfillment. Sometimes it is and sometimes not. The kings Saul and Solomon got worse with age; Jacob and Paul got better."[15]

When persons come to a point that they recognize that aging is a natural process of life and admit that they are in that process, they are on the way to successful aging. When Paul stated that he had lived a full life, fought the good fight, and was finishing the course, he was stating that he had lived a fulfilled life.[16] All need personal fulfillment to accept the totality of life.

Personal fulfillment really comes only in the extension of years. People fear death because death cuts off life. Why do individuals have the fear? Possibly it is because subconsciously they are aware that they have not achieved what they feel they should have in life.

They have not been fulfilled. For the Christian, the fulfilled life is not obtaining material things or receiving earthly honors. These things are not wrong in themselves, if held in proper perspective. The bottom line for senior

Christians is whether they have attempted obedience to God's will throughout life, after accepting Christ Jesus as Savior and Lord.

This writer believes that the Christian life can be one of fulfillment at any stage if persons are living in fellowship with their Lord. However, would not life be more meaningful if they are allowed to live extended lives and mature in the fruits of the spirit? Jesus said, *"I have come that they may have life and have it to the full."*[17]

To experience successful aging personally, all need to grasp the principle that it is the whole life – all the stages – that is going to give the fulfillment of this wonderful promise of Jesus. As stated in the opening section of this chapter, for a person to age successfully, he needs to fear God. In addition, man needs to have a continuing dependence on God.

In addition, man also needs to have a continuing dependence on God. *"Even to your old age and gray hairs, I am He; I am He who will sustain you. I have made you and I will carry you; I will sustain you, and I will rescue."*[18] This is a wonderful promise that enables individuals to depend upon God all the days of their lives. Aging successfully means exhibiting that kind of dependence.

Old age is a time for honor and respect. If people's days are to be long upon the earth, then they must honor their fathers and their mothers.[19] Moses was more than likely speaking to adults who had parents who were older. So this commandment applied to them as well as children who had younger parents. *"Listen to your fathers who gave you life, and do not despise your mother when she is old."*[20]

There are many references in the scriptures about respecting and honoring older persons: *"Rise in the presence of the aged. Show respect for the elderly, and revere your Lord. I am the Lord."*[21] *"Do not rebuke an older man harshly, but exhort him as if he were your father. Treat younger men as brothers, older women as mothers, and younger women as sisters with absolute purity.*[22]

Church members should be aware of the older persons in their midst and use wisdom from these elders for the good of Christ and His church. In the planning of programs, particularly those dealing with senior adults, the seniors of a church should be consulted. They should be given responsibility for conducting their own activities. The church needs their wisdom. *"Ask your Father and He will tell you; your elders, and they will explain to you."*[23]

There must be progressive spiritual growth in people's lives as long as they continue to live. A pastor, senior adult minister, Sunday School teachers, or other leaders need to be obedient to Paul's teaching: *"We proclaim Him, admonishing, and teaching everyone with all wisdom so that we may present everyone perfect in Christ."*[24]

To present every person before God perfect in Christ is a life-long pursuit. It is a never ending task. When thinking of ministry with senior adults, church leaders should recognize the need for continuing growth. Recognizing that there may be some decline, physical or otherwise, among these seniors, there still needs to be continuing spiritual growth. The leaders of the church are to use their gifts in a responsible way to seize opportunities to help perfect the senior adults.

It's interesting to examine the scriptures and see how they relate to the process of aging in this modern day. This short study of some of the perspectives in aging reveals that there are many foundations contained within the scriptures on which a church can build a ministry to and with aging persons.

Chapter 8
Endnotes

1. Rolf P. Knierim, "Age and Aging in the Old Testament," in *Ministry with the Aging*, ed. William M. Clements (New York: Harper & Row, 1981), p. 21.
2. Ecclesiastes 3:1-2.
3. Psalms 90:10.
4. Jeremiah 6:11.
5. 1 Kings 3:14.
6. Genesis 15:15.
7. Job 12:12.
8. Numbers 11:16.
9. Psalms 71:9.
10. Genesis 48:10.
11. Deuteronomy 34:7.
12. 2Samuel 9.
13. Proverbs 10:27.
14. Joshua 23:2.
15. Stagg, *The Bible Speaks on Aging*, pp. 178-179.
16. 2 Timothy 4:7.
17. John 10:10.
18. Isaiah 46:3-4.
19. Exodus 26:12.
20. Proverbs 23:22.
21. Leviticus 20.22.
22. 1 Timothy 5:12.
23. Deuteronomy 32:7.
24. Colossians 1:28.

Chapter 9
Death And Dying

Death and dying is a subject which holds deep interest for aging persons. David asked this question, *"What man can live and not see death or save himself from the power of the grave?"*[1] Death is an experience that not a living person or thing avoid – the second coming of the Lord Christ Jesus will eliminate death for the Christian of that time. Even with the certainty of this event always lurking around, society attempts to ignore the subject of death and dying.

Unfortunately, it is not only society in general who has a problem in dealing with dying and death; Christians, in spite of their belief of life after death, have more difficulty with dying than they are ready to admit. Regardless of one's credits or fame, death is a certainty.

More thought about the unthinkable needs to occur in our society and the church. Also needed is more education and preparation in the field of thanatology, i.e. the study of death and dying. The church should begin properly equipping he body of believers with a basic theology of death.

This chapter has the purpose of helping people to begin to accept death as a fact of life. When Christians accept this truth, then they can begin to view it as another stage in the total life cycle – death as simply another transition. The Christian then enters the stage of everlasting life, which is to be enjoyed forever.

Death In Greek and Old Testament Thought

The Greek word Thanatos means the act of dying or the state of death.[2] Colin Brown relates that for the Greeks death was the living activity, the destruction of existence. Death is something that is certain to happen, and since they didn't have a doctrine of creation, they didn't question the fact of death. The Greeks believed in living life to its fullest; death after a full life was a blessing, a release from the futilities of life.[3] However, death was a problem, but they solved it by thinking they lived on in their children. The Greeks liked to die gloriously on the field of battle.

The Stoics, regarding themselves in the process of dying, had little fear of it and felt they needed no liberation from the power of death. They felt one who was overcome by death and the fear of it was one who was really dead.[4]

Gnosticism was a sharp, antithetical cosmic dualism. The cosmos is no good and the body is part of the cosmos. The soul was light and life and is only imprisoned in the body. The soul is liberated from the body, and this is victory over death.[5]

In Old Testament thought when death comes, it is the final end of man's existence. Death itself is not feared. It is early death that is of concern; they felt that early death was God's punishment for a person's guilt. It was by this early death that God cleansed the community of those doing wrong. It was in this way that the community sentenced individuals to death so that the community wouldn't be judged:

> "Death itself is not a divine punishment, since it was not part of the intention of creation that man should be immortal. Adam was

threatened with early death as a punishment for a definite act of disobedience; after the fall had taken place, he was punished merely by exclusion from the garden of Eden...

"Although there is thus mention of the universality of sin and death (the only exceptions being the cases of "translation"), there is in the Old Testament as little mention of inherited death as a consequence of sin and death of Adam as there is of original sin. Since God's relationship is not primarily with individuals, but with people (covenant = Israel), death does not represent a threat to faith, and the question "why?" does not arrive with regard to death."[6]

After the time of the exile, the thinking of the people and the covenant of Yahweh had new meaning. The main belief was in the Torah, and a person had more of an individual relationship with God. Death began to be thought of altogether as punishment for sin:

"Where death is thus regarded not as a natural destiny of man, but is something brought upon him in the course of history, the way is open for reflection upon the possibility that God will overcome sin and death. Thus in Jewish apocalyptic, we find the concept of a Kingdom of God as the end of time, in which sin has been conquered and death has lost its power. The hope of resurrection, first found in Isaiah 26:19 and Daniel 12:2, and then formulated with the help of Iranian ideas, further makes possible a faith and even for earlier generations death will be overcome by divine act of new creation. The righteous will enter into eternal life, the unrighteous into eternal death. The doctrine of resurrection naturally remained a subject of controversy. The

Pharisees defended it and were opposed by the Sadducees. There were also differing opinions as to whether only Israelites will be resurrected, or also Gentiles, only the righteous or also the unrighteous (the latter to judgment)."[7]

Death In The New Testament

The New Testament view of death is a continuation of the old Jewish view. Death is always seen as a death of the individual. Since this is the case, it is important to determine what causes death. Paul provides the answer: *"For the wages of sin is death."*[8] From this view, Satan is the one having power over death.

It is, of course, God Himself who can destroy both body and soul in hell. Throughout the New Testament the question as to the cause of death is not one of speculation. Paul, in guarding against the idea that death has simply been a fate inherited, says that death has spread to all men. *"Because all have sinned."* Death is the punishment for each man's sins; all men without exception, are subject to sin and death.

Victory over death, salvation, and life cannot come as a result of man's own efforts. Salvation comes; life comes through an act of God's grace and can only be appropriated by man.

"From all that we have said, it is evident that in the New Testament death is regarded not as a natural process, but as a historical event, indicating clearly the sinful condition of man...Jesus died our human death (Philippians 2:2), and He really died it, as the "buried" of the early confession indicates (1 Corinthians 15:3). This death is "for us," i.e., to our advantage, a teaching which is emphasized in various ways by statements about His resurrection and exaltation. His death overcomes the law, and our death. It is to make manifest this victory that the death of Jesus, the risen, present and coming One, is proclaimed, in order that His death may not have been in vain."[9] The intention in the New Testament is to declare that God breaks the power of sin when He identifies Himself with man in the death of Christ Jesus therein breaking the death of the law, ending the validity of the law, and then taking away the power of death. The New Testament emphasizes that the sting of death will never be felt by the Christian believer because it was experienced by Christ on the cross on behalf of all. Death only leads the Christian into eternal fellowship with the One who experienced the sting of death.

Acceptance of Death

Paul Tournier asked a question which all believers need to examine. "Is acceptance of old age and death easier for believers than for unbelievers?"[10] Tournier does not in all honesty think he can give a "Yes" answer.[11] Tournier believes that the acceptance of old age and death is more of a psychological problem than a religious one regardless of the appearances:[12]

> "In the last analysis all anxiety is reduced to anxiety about death. Proof of this is the large number of stories in which a man freed from the fear of death is seen to be free from all other fears: he has no fear of anything or anyone; no one can overcome him, even by killing him. Nevertheless, the sociologists are right: men do not talk much about

this anxiety concerning the threat of death. This is because all men attempt to repress it."[13]

People talk about the subject but do most anything other than discuss the latent anxiety that is crying to get out:

> "People are reluctant to talk about old age and death, because they are afraid of emotion, and they willingly avoid the things they feel most emotional about, though these are the very things they feel most emotional about, though these are the very things they most need to talk about."[14]

The writers of many books want to destroy the taboo on old age. They write many words about destroying the myths and stereotypes in ageism. Tournier asked an important question.:

"Can one really abolish the taboo on old age without also abolishing the taboo on death? This seems to me to be one of the requirements of our time. We aspire to looking everything in the face, bringing everything out into the open.

The sex taboo has been overthrown. It is desired to abolish a taboo on old age. But the taboo on death is in the same basket.[15] "When a man looks for meaning in his life, when an old person looks for the meaning of his old age, they are really, underneath, asking about the meaning of death. Who can deny that the meaning of life is death, since it is a journey whose final destination is death.[16]

"Now the meaning of death is the religious question par excellence. Does there exist something other than the visible world in which we are enclosed from birth to death? Something which transcends death, which sets beyond death the destination of the journey of life? My old age has meaning; I can live through it with my gaze still fixed before me, and not behind me, because I am on my way to a destination beyond death."[17]

In modern society individuals may ask, "Why death?" The Christian needs to believe the same answer that Paul does, therefore, just as sin entered the world through one man, and death through sin, and then this way death came to all men.[18] Death and sin are close kin. Death is no friend of man. Death is the enemy. This sounds so final, but for the Christian it isn't . The scripture teach that without death there can be no life. The kernel of wheat must die so it can live.[19]

Believers enthusiastically speak about the glorious even that happened on the day we call Easter, but sometimes I the glory of it all they forget about Good Friday. I heard an older preacher give a moving sermon on just four words, repeating them over and over and over again with different emphasis: "Friday's here – Sunday's comin'; Friday's here – Sunday's comin'." To experience Easter Sunday means accepting the experience of Good Friday. Death must happen to Christians so they can get on with eternal life.

Causes Of Death

What are the main causes of death in our society? Today in the United States, three of four persons sixty-five or older die from **heart disease, cancer and stroke alone.** Heart disease is a number one cause of death for all age groups – including the elderly – far outranking any other cause of death. However, over the last decade deaths due to cardiovascular disease and stroke decreased, but those due to cancer (malignant neoplasm) increased.[20]

Because of illness does not terminate lives as early as it has in the past, people have longer to develop an awareness of impending death. Individuals in the process of dying have a right to know their limited time.

Who is being protected? Is it the dying person or the doctor, staff, and family? It is not unusual to see persons who think right up to the last minutes that they are going to live and then go into a coma, then death. In a number of these cases there were some things that these aging, dying person would have said or done if they had known for sure they were dying. Someone may say there is always hope; true, but that hope would be there as well if the persons knew they were dying. The next context discussed is that of "suspicion awareness":

> "The patient is neither ignorant nor aware of the true circumstances. He suspects that he is going to die but does not know for sure. What happens when the staff knows but conceals and the patient suspects? The most common event is a contest, a contest for the control of information. The patient desires confirmation of a suspicion. He needs evidence, and so must either detect or elicit signs that will confirm his suspicions.
>
> "What are the consequences...? But the important thing to realize is that suspicion awareness is highly unstable. The patient usually oscillates between more or less suspicion. His spirits go up and down. He may even convert to another type of awareness."[21]

This context is as bad, if not worse, than closed awareness. It puts pressure on everyone concerned with the patient. It creates feelings of guilt among the caring family as they duck questions from the dying person or just plain lie when asked a direct question "Am I going to die?" A pastor of a person in a suspicion context has to watch every word for the sake of the family- notice I said the family, not the patient. A pastor is not doing any favors for the patient at this point. When the pastor prays, again each word must be guarded because the patient is just looking for some hint to justify his suspicion. The suspicion context in contrast to the closed context may at least give the dying person time to take some cautionary measures, like drawing up a will or making some verbal request.

There is a third type of awareness context called the "ritual drama of mutual pretense":

> "This occurs when both patient and staff know that the patient is dying and both agree to act as if he were going to live. The researchers characterize the interaction as a masquerade. It is an informal drama in which the script is written as the play proceeds. There is an extensive use of props. Masks: these hide the facial expressions which are appropriate to the real situation. Costumes: patients dress for the part of not-dying, paying special attention to good grooming. Stage sets: fixing up the room so that it's just like home. Both the patient and the staff cooperate in the use of these props to maintain the pretense."[22]

This context may have many beneficial effects. The person involved may feel good if all goes well. A feeling of satisfaction may occur. There are also many negatives effects. I may become harder to hide increasing pain. The growing grief within the family members may remove the masks they are wearing. It may come to a point where family members ignore or at least give the dying person a feeling of being in a state of isolation. The dying person then experiences what Larry Richards calls "social death":

> "There are pressures on the medical staff, on the family, on friends, and on ministers which, though often unrecognized, have a traumatic impact on relationships with the terminally ill. All too often these unrecognized reactions and the failure of those in the caring community to work through their own attitudes and needs resulted in something that has been called "social death." There is a gradual, unintended and yet deeply painful stripping away the personhood of the terminally ill person. He is treated in many ways as if he was already dead."[23]

This writer has on more than one occasion been in the presence of a person considered "socially dead." When attempts were made to ask the dying person a question, one of the family members answered without giving the patient an opportunity.

Persons in the room, particularly close family members, talked about the patient as if he were non-existent, let alone able to hear anything. During some of these encounters, the eyes of a brother known for a few years and the expression of his face have reflected hurt. It is as if he is saying, "What's the use of fighting for life? They consider me nonexistent anyway." When the personhood is stripped away, actual death generally is not far away.

The final context, and personally the most acceptable is called "open awareness." However, this approach is not without problems. Is there anything that has been brought about as a result of sin without problems? Is there anything that has been brought about as a result of sin without problems? Neale says that: "...both patient and staff know that he is dying and both acknowledge the fact. It is clear that this context eliminates some of the problems created by the other three. Yet we should not minimize the problems involved."[24]

During this context many questions will be asked about the mode of dying and when the actual death will occur. Now that these persons know they are going to die and others also know this, the question remains how they go about dying? How are they going to present themselves to the world? They want others, particularly close family members, to witness them dying with decent composure and with as much dignity as possible.

All of these four awareness contexts need to be recognized so people can minister both to the terminally ill patients and the family members. Even with the dangers of the open awareness context, ministering in this setting is easier.

Neale closes this section on awareness by asking three questions:

"Do we make too much or too little of death? Is awareness of our own death even possible? Is awareness of death useful? There are no definite answers. Perhaps this is because we have not yet learned how to ask the questions, or it may be that the better the question, the less likely the possibility of answeres."[25]

Grief And Its Stages

Kubler-Ross has conducted mountains of research on death and had many interviews with persons facing death. She has identified five stages of grief which a dying person goes through.

The first of these stages is **denial**.[26] When individuals become terminally ill, they deny it by going about as if nothing was happening for a period of time. They will find all kinds of reasons why it can't be true. Sometimes denial is a buffer to protect dying persons from having to deal with a painful situation. "We cannot look at the sun all the time; we cannot face death all the time."[27] "Denial is usually a temporary defense and soon will be replaced by partial acceptance."[28]

The second stage is **anger**. "When the first state of denial cannot be maintained any longer, it is replaced by feelings of anger, rage, envy and resentment. The logical next question becomes: "Why me?"[29] The dying project anger onto all within reach. This anger is very difficult for caring persons to cope with.

"The third stage is **bargaining**, which is less well known but equally helpful to the patient, but only for brief periods of time."[30] After acceptance that death may occur, then the patients may attempt to make an agreement which may postpone the final moment. Bargaining generally involves a reward and also has a self-imposed deadline.[31]

The fourth stage is **depression** which come as a result of the loss the dying is experiencing.[32]

Finally, if there has been enough time and if the dying have had support I working through their grief, they may reach some degree of **acceptance:**

"Acceptance should not be mistaken for a happy stage. It is almost void of feelings. It is as if the pain had gone, and the struggle is over, and there comes a time for "the final rest before the long journey" as one patient phrased it. This is also a time during which the family usually needs more help, understanding, and support than the patient himself."[33]

Fear of Death

How about older Christians facing death? They seem to accept it better than a younger person. Do older persons fear death? Even though they dread the thought of a prolonged terminal illness more, they still fear death in the sense they don't want it. It is human nature not to want to die. Jesus was God. Jesus was human as we are, yet without sin.

Jesus didn't want to die. The prayer in the garden of Gethsemane was not a casual, "Father, if it be possible, let this cup pass from me." No, He prayed that prayer three times while the sweat formed on his forehead like great globules of blood.

Each time the disciples had time enough to go back to sleep. No, Jesus did not want to die. But in perfect obedience to the will of the Father, He turned His face toward Jerusalem to experience death and make it possible for the Christian to view death only as a transitory stage.

There seemingly is a fear of dying in all humans. Fearing death does not mean that people are any less Christian or that they lack spiritual development; Christians fear death because they fear dying. They fear it because they are not taught how to handle dying.

Robert Neale identifies three major fears. "The first category of fears includes those which relate to what happens after death occurs."[34] There are three kinds of fears in this category, **the first being about the fate of the body.**[35] Mankind worship their bodies.

The body is important in this society, and all seem concerned about its fate. Believers know the Bible teaches that they are going to be absent from the body, and it is going back to dust. However, because of cultural and societal values, there is reluctance to give up the body.

The thought may be working in the far corner of people's minds that they may need their bodies or parts of them in Heaven. Maybe this is the reason that there are not many organ donors.

Another example of people's reverence of the body can be seen when they parade into the funeral home and admire the body of the deceased. "Doesn't he look good?" "Didn't they do a nice job on him?" "It doesn't look like her." "They have made her look nicer than she ever looked." "What a terrible job; I wouldn't bring anybody to this funeral home, and don't you dare bring me here." Our society, at least sections of it, admire the body right down to the final inspection. The fate of the body causes fear.

"A second fear relating to what happens after death is fear of the judgement."[36] It makes no difference what a person's religious persuasion is; there is fear of the judgment.

"The final fear in this category pertains to the unknown."[37] The scripture tells us that there are mysteries. Humans only see through a glass dimly. They do not know everything that is going to happen. In trust and faith believers can be confident that there will be a time when there will be no more tears or sadness, and they will be faced to face with Jesus. But there are many things they aren't sure about. There are many unanswered questions. The unknown always brings about a certain amount of apprehension.

The next step is a turn "from the fear of what happens after death to the category or fear related to the process of dying. Fear of the process is quite different from the fear just described."[38]

The first category is pain. "Death = pain = fear."[39] Whenever people think of death, they think of pain; and when they think of pain, they think of fear. This may be because there is little opportunity in this society to experience pain. Only those persons who have a severe arthritic problem or some other affliction that causes deep pain really know what pain is like. If it gets too hot or too cold, the thermostat is adjusted. If people experience a headache, the television ad tells all kinds of remedies and how fast each will work. Whatever the problem, there is a cure. This society does not tolerate pain of any kind because pain is feared.

"A second fear about the process of dying is the fear of indignity. Some are ashamed to participate in dying."[40] For example, terminally ill women as well as others, always want to look their best for their visiting pastor or other friends. They make excuses about the way they look. They desire to go to the hairdresser. They want to use their makeup. The terminally ill want to look their best for the important persons in their lives. And, of course, they can't. There is a fear about the process of dying because of the indignity that it brings to the life of a person; they don't want to be remembered by their debilitated condition.

"The final fear in the category is the fear of being a burden. There is no question about the fact that many are likely to be burdens. Few die by accident, and modern medicine prolongs the dying process."[41] Talking about being a burden means being a physical, an emotional, or financial burden.

This is a very real fear for many persons. It is very common for a minister to hear, "I don't want to be a burden on my family or anybody."

"**The final category is that many persons fear death as a loss of life.** First in this category is the loss of mastery."[42] Death represents the end of control over life. People desire to control themselves, control others, and to control their life situations. When they are dying, they have almost no control.

"**The second fear of death as a loss of life is related to incompleteness and failure.**"[43] Persons have goals to reach. Death is no respecter of those goals. Many become angry because death is going to prevent them from finishing something they have started.

"**Finally we fear death because it means separation**. This is a most common and most complicated fear."[44] People like to do things with someone else. They have a very difficult time doing anything by themselves. Loss by death means separation. Accepting the fact that it is temporary for the Christian doesn't make it any less a fear:

> "After this review of three categories and nine examples of fear, you should have some awareness of the fears of your own response to death. Which fear or fears or other fears best describe your situations?"[45]

All people have a fear or fears. Before they can minister to others, they are going to have to come to terms with their fears in a satisfactory way.

Activities Concerning Death Of The Aging

In this society there are common attitudes toward the dying and death of an older person. One is that aged persons are really, if not actually, longing for the final event. It's a myth. They want to live as much as anyone else. The statement is made that those who have lived sixty-five years have lived a long life. It's the quality. When Christians have one more day of life, it's another day they can serve the Lord.

Another statement is made on a more philosophical level, but it is just as untrue. Death is natural and timely for old persons; and it's the thing to happen when people begin to age. Even though it may be a social loss when the elderly die, society doesn't take their death too seriously. When people read in the obituary column that an infant or a young person dies, they say, "What a tragedy!" But if a seventy year old person dies, it's not considered too important. The loss is felt, but there is a difference in the sense of loss.

When dealing with older dying persons, caring individuals need to understand that the age is not the major factor to be dealt with, but the condition causing the death. There is too much emphasis on chronological age. Age doesn't necessarily determine how to minister or relate to a person. Many other things need to be taken into consideration.

Some older persons will say death is preferable to inactivity. Some others say death is preferable to the loss of mental faculties. Church members need to understand these feelings so that when an older person to whom they are ministering responds differently than they anticipate, they can accept what is said with grace. Those who minister need to be understanding and empathize with these older persons in terms of where they are coming from.

Effective Caring Attitudes

How can caring people be more effective in their ministry to the older dying person? George Patterson, in *Ministry With the Aging*, presents four principles he adheres to in his ministry.

"The first is simply to be there. The most valuable thing to offer to the older aging person is a caring presence."[46] This doesn't mean that a great amount of time is required during a visit; it does mean there should be frequent visits to the person who is experiencing the dying process. When there, ministering persons should be there. The person needs their full attention. Other things should be secondary.

The second principle recommended is to be natural.[47] Those visitors should not wear a mask. They shouldn't act like they have all the answers. They should be what they have been with the person in the past.

The third principle is to listen.[48] One of the greatest problems for all people is to listen to what others are saying. Most people are generally too occupied with what they are going to say that they don't listen to what is being said. If they listen attentively, they can also pick up on feeling as well as words. When they are not tuned in to what the dying person is really saying, they fail to perform quality ministry:

> "The final principle I follow is to try to understand, to perceive as fully as possible the ideas, attitudes and feelings of the other person.
>
> "...Often we are so anxious to change the dying person that we don't take time to try and understand him or her."[49]

Caring is reflected simply by affirmation, a touch, a smile, an arm around a shoulder, or just being there and not saying or doing anything.

In conclusion, it should be remembered that death for Christians is never faced alone. Jesus is with them; He understands them; He has been part of their lives from the moment of their acceptance of His love relationship. Jesus also understands death, the pain and anguish of the events before the final moment. He experienced it. Christians have a friend, a brother, a Savior, a Lord who walks all the way through the door of the shadow with them. That is not all. He welcomes believers into the future that He made possible and there is a companion throughout eternity. *"Where, O death, is your victory? Where, O death, is your sting?"*[50]

Chapter 9
Endnotes

1. Psalms 89:48.
2. Colin Brown, ed., *The New International Dictionary of New Testament Theology*, 3 vols. (Grand Rapids: Zondervan Publishing House, 1979), 1:430.
3. Ibid., p. 431.
4. Ibid.
5. Ibid., p. 432.
6. Ibid., p. 433.
7. Ibid., p. 434.
8. Romans 6:23.
9. Colin Brown, *Dictionary of New Testament Theology*, p. 451.
10. Paul Tournier, *Learning to Grow Old* (New York: Harper & Row, Publishers, 1972), p. 218.
11. Ibid., p. 219.
12. Ibid., p. 219.

13. Ibid.,p. 216.
14. Ibid.
15. Ibid.,p. 218.
16. Ibid., p. 219.
17. Ibid.
18. Romans 5:12.
19. John 12:24.
20. *Aging America: Trends and Projection* (Report from U. S. Special Committee on Aging, 1984), p. 55.
21. Ibid., pp. 15-16.
22. Ibid., p. 17.
23. Larry Richards and Paul Johnson, Death & The Caring Community (Portland: Multnormal Press, 1980), p. 67.
24. Neal, *The Art of Dying*, p. 18.
25. Ibid., p.22.
26. Elizabeth Kubler-Ross, *On Death and Dying* (New York: MacMillian Publishing Co., Inc.), p. 38.
27. Ibid., p. 39.
28. Ibid., p. 40.
29. Ibid., p. 50.
30. Ibid., p. 82.
31. Ibid., p. 83.
32. Ibid., p. 85.
33. Ibid., p. 113.
34. Neale, *The Art of Dying*, p. 31.
35. Ibid.
36. Ibid.

37. Ibid.

38. Ibid., p. 32.

39. Ibid.

40. Ibid., p. 33.

41. Ibid.

42. Ibid.

43. Ibid., p. 34.

44. Ibid.

45. Ibid., p. 35.

46. George Patterson, "Death, Dying, and the Elderly," in *Ministry With the Aging*, ed. William M. Clements (New York: Harper & Row, Publishers, 1981), p. 230.

47. Ibid., p. 231.

48. Ibid.

49. Ibid., p. 232.

50. 1 Corinthians 15:55.

Chapter 10
Conclusion

This has been an educational and rewarding experience studying the process of aging. Hopefully you will now have a better understanding of this process and discard the myths that may have caused someone you know to go through it not enjoyable.

Aging is a life-long process; it will invade all of us who continue to live; so make or get the best out of your years. The choice is yours.

I have been enlightened, hopefully you have too.

Joseph R. Rogers, Sr.

Selected Bibliography

Agruso, Victor M. *Learning In The Later Years*. New York: Academic Press, 1978.

Butler, Robert N., and Lewis, Mryna I. *Aging & Mental Health*. New York: New American Library, 1973.

Clements, William M. *Ministry With The Aging*. New York: Harper & Row, 1981.

_____. *Care And Counseling Of The Aging*. Philadelphia: Fortress Press, 1979.

Collins, Gary R. *Christian Counseling: A Comprehensive Guide*. Waco: Word Books, 1980.

Donahue, Wilma. *Education Or Later Maturity*. New York: Whiteside, Inc., 1955.

Dye, Harold E. *No Rocking Chair For Me!*. Nashville: Broadman Press, 1975.

Freeman, Carroll B. *The Senior Adult Years*. Nashville: Broadman Press, 1979.

Gaebelein, Frank E., gen. ed. *The Expositor's Bible Commentary*. Grand Rapids: Zondervan Publishing House, 1976.

Grosheide, F. W. *Commentary On The First Epistle To The Corinthians*. Grand Rapids: Wm. B. Eerdman's Publishing Co., 1953.

Hart, Archibald D. *Depression: Coping And Caring*. Arcadia: Cope Publications, 1981.

Howell, John C. *Senior Adult Family Life*. Nashville: Broadman Press, 1979.

Janss, Edmund. *Making The Second Half the Best Half*. Minneapolis: Bethany House Publishers, 1984.

Kubler-Ross, Elizabeth. *On Death And Dying*. New York: Macmillian Publishing Co., 1969.
_____. *Living With Death And Dying*. New York: Macmillan Co., 1981.

Madden, Myron, and Madden, Mary Ben. *The Time Of Your Life*. Nashville: Broadman Press, 1977.

_____. *For Grandparents Wonders And Worries*. Philadelphia: The Westminister Press, 1980.

Neale, Robert E. *The Art Of Dying*. New York: Harper & Row, Publishers, 1973.

Pearson, Durk, and Saw, Sandy. *Life Extension*. New York: Warner Books, Inc., 1981.

Pesmen, Curtis. *How A Man Ages*. New York: Ballatine Books, 1984.

Poreino, Jane. *Growing Older, Getting Better*. Reading: Addison-Wesley Publishing Company, 1983.

Richards, Larry, and Johnson, Paul. *Death & The Caring Community*. Portland: Multnormal Press, 1980.

Sessons, Bob. *150 Ideas For Activities With Senior Adults*. Nashville: Broadman Press, 1977.

Skinner, B. F., and Vaughan, M. E. *Enjoy Old Age*. New York: W. W. Norton & Company, 1983.

Tourneir, Paul. *Learn To Grow Old*. New York: Harper & Row, Publishers, 1983.

UPDATE
Mrs. Pearlie Graham Rogers

Pearlie Graham Rogers was born in Florence County, South Carolina on **May 18, 1912** to the late Viola & Joe Graham. Her early years of development were spent in the same county. After her **adolescent years** her family moved to Williamsburg County in the same state.

It was there that she was united in holy matrimony to the late **Willie Rogers, Jr. of Sylvania, Georgia**. This year they would have celebrated **seventy-three (73)** years of marital blitz if my father was still living. While residing in South Carolina eight of their fourteen were born.

My mother had **three (3) sisters and two (2) brothers**. All of my mother's brothers and sisters lived beyond **the age of sixty (60)**. She has one brother still living**, Herbert Graham**, in Florence, South Carolina.

In the **middle forties (1946)** the family relocated to Middlesex, (Nash County) North Carolina and the remaining **six of the siblings were born**. My mother did have one still birth, which she does not talk much about. During these years the family's main source of income was sharecropping (tobacco, corn and cotton).

My mother was not able to obtain a **good education** because in that period of time blacks were not allowed to be educated with the basis – reading, writing and arithmetic. Other obligations and **responsibilities** in the home also **contributed** to this cause. She only completed the **third grade**. Yet, in spite of the oppositions she still **functioned excellent as a mother**.

In 1957 her beloved husband passed away and left her with the responsibility of rearing and nurturing the **siblings (12)**; (the other two were living with other relatives). By the grace and mercy of the Lord, she did an outstanding job as mother and father. She did not remarry because she said, **"I don't want my children calling another person, daddy."**

In 1959 Pearlie had a *vision* from the Lord to join the senior choir at the Stokes Chapel Missionary Baptist Church of Middlesex, North Carolina. During this experience with the Lord, she voiced her concerns about not being able to **read properly**. But as she tells it, the Lord was not interested in **listening to excuses**. At the present time she reads well.

During this encounter she remembers very vividly her body slowly, slowly moving toward what she believed to **be physical death**. But once she said, **"Yes"** to the Lord, she began to feel her body being **revived**. Since this encounter to this present day **(2005)** she is **active singing in the adult choir**.

My mother is a role model to her **family**, her **church** and her **community**. Her **legacy** will forever be **embossed** in the hearts and minds of many people. Who better is there to share some **insights about the process of life from a physical/biblical perspective (The Joy of Aging)** than this able and qualified young lady?

- o She has never spent a day in the **hospital because of sickness**.
- o She has never had a **complete physical examination**.
- o She has never taken **hormones**.
- o She does not drink **coffee, tea, carbonated sodas or juice – just water**.

As of this writing she **(93)** does not take **any prescription medications**. She has had **cataracts surgery (in doctor's office)**. I remember the doctor asking for **her medical history**, but we had to tell him that she did not have any.

In closing, I admire my mother for her **courage, strength, temperament, love** and **faith**. Even though she is **a very modest person**, **this daughter, wife, mother, friend** and **role model** has allowed the Lord to use her in a wonderful way.

She has been privileged to live **two millenniums** (1900 & 2000), **two centuries** (20th & 21st), World Wars I & II, Vietnam, Korea & Japan Conflict, Desert Storm and the latest Iraqi War.

My mother has been privileged to live during the terms of fifteen (**15**) **U.S. Presidents: William Howard Taft – George W. Bush**. She has also been privileged to live during the terms of twenty **(20) North Carolina Governors: William Walton Kitchin – Michael F. Easley**.

Who is better **qualified** to share some **insights and truths about aging**, **but Pearlie Graham Rogers**? It is because of my admiration for her and her life that I share this important information with you. It is my hope that after you read this book, you will be inspired to appreciate life and thank God for every moment He allowed you to live.

So, my friend, never fear **"Aging"**, it is the normal process of life.

Joseph R. Rogers, Sr., D. Min.

Author's Contacts And Other Works

Mailing Address:
1313 Ujamaa Drive, Raleigh, NC 27610
Phone Nos. (919) 208-0200, (919) 829-7179

Email Address:
jroger3420@aol.com,
jrrphila1428@aol.com

Websites:
Ormanpress.com, or lulu.com

Notes